REPEATABIL

CHRIS ZOOK ▸ JAMES ALLEN

BAIN & COMPANY, INC.

REPEATABILITY

Build Enduring
Businesses
for a World of
Constant Change

HARVARD BUSINESS REVIEW PRESS

Boston, Massachusetts

Net Promoter® score, Net Promoter®, and NPS® are registered trademarks of Bain & Company, Inc., Fred Reichheld, and Satmetrix Systems, Inc.

RAPID® is a registered trademark of Bain & Company, Inc.

Library of Congress Cataloging-in-Publication Data

Zook, Chris, 1951–
  Repeatability : build enduring businesses for a world of constant change / Chris Zook and James Allen.
    p. cm.
  ISBN 978-1-4221-4330-8 (alk. paper)
 1. Strategic planning. 2. Business planning. 3. Technological innovation.
4. Organizational change. 5. Performance. I. Allen, James, 1960– II. Title.
  HD30.28.Z66 2012
  658.4'012—dc23

                                                                    2011029764

The paper used in this publication meets the requirements of the American National Standard for Permanence of Paper for Publications and Documents in Libraries and Archives Z39.48-1992.

Contents

Introduction

What you see depends on where you sit. If you are high in the stadium at a tennis match, you see the angles and patterns of strategy, but miss the violent physicality of professional tennis on the ground. At courtside, you see the physicality, but at the cost of the angles and positioning. And only on the court itself, in the action, do you have a full sense of the speed of the ball, and the fact that only through almost instant reactions, with repeatable and well-grooved response patterns, can any strategy be successful at the highest level of the game.

In our combined careers, we have logged more than fifty years in the business of strategy consulting, shoulder to shoulder with senior executives of global companies. For about twenty-five years of that time, we have been privileged to lead the Global Strategy practice of Bain & Company, examining the broad patterns of business success and failure. We have also been part of teams starting and managing businesses. Each position has given us a different slant on the topic of how companies find their next wave of profitable growth. Today, each is leading us to the single insight at the center of this book—the growing power of repeatable models.

During the last ten years, we have led a research project at Bain on this topic, reported on in a series of articles and books with Harvard Business Review Press. The books, called "the trilogy" by our publisher, looked at the three ways that companies grow (or fail to do so). These are through growth in market share and profit share in the core, growth from expansion into surrounding adjacent markets, and, sometimes, redefinition of the business model itself. We called this the *focus-expand-redefine* cycle of growth.

Yet, only after we had looked at the success factors of companies from so many different angles—both personal and research-based—did we see how the nature of strategy in business itself is changing fundamentally. What once were more lasting sources of competitive advantage—like market positioning, a unique product offering, a powerful brand, or a set of deep customer relationships—have, in many industries, become more ephemeral and fleeting, to the point where, at the time of this writing, we calculate that only about 9 percent of global companies have been able to achieve more than a modest level of sustained and profitable growth over the course of the last decade.

The nature of successful strategy is changing in three ways. First, it is now much less about a detailed plan than about a general direction and a few critical initiatives—almost a strategy on a page—built around deep capabilities that can be constantly improved, adapted, and reapplied. The reason for this is the increased speed at which information flows and change occurs in the world, compressing time. These changes are shifting the nature of competitive advantage toward deep capabilities and how they combine in a business model that can adapt and repeat successes of the past over and over.

Second, strategy is now less about anticipating how the world will change, which is increasingly difficult to know, than about superiority at rapid testing, learning, changing, and adapting.

Some of the great stall-outs of recent years, such as at Nokia, have occurred because of failure to adapt to change. Some of the most powerful success stories, such as at Apple, have been fueled by best-in-class systems to test, gain feedback, and adapt. Central to this responsiveness, we find, is the ability to maintain a level of simplicity of the business model (for instance, Apple has only about sixty products) in an increasingly complex world.

Third, effective strategy is becoming increasingly indistinguishable from an effective organization. The best strategies are those that the organization readily embraces, mobilizes around quickly, and provides feedback on. Such strategies almost feel as if they were pulled up from the bottom rather than pushed down from the top. When the full organization understands deeply the strategy, its ability to learn and adjust to change will have a good chance at being better than competitors'. We refer to this result as *shortening the distance* between the CEO, the front line, and the customer.

A central insight from this book is that complexity has become the silent killer of growth strategies—complexity of organizations layered with constant new initiatives and systems, complexity of messages throughout the organization, complexity of implementation across different markets, complexity of IT systems to keep track of it all. Complexity creeps up on companies, confounds learning, slows response time, and saps organizational and management energy. It is a truism that from the first product sold by the founder to his first customer, the complexity of most businesses grows exponentially, drawing senior management farther and farther away from the front line.

It is no wonder that our CEO surveys and interviews highlight the tension CEOs feel between speed of markets (and therefore the need to respond) and complexity (and therefore slowness) of organizations. Some said that by the time they are partway through implementing a major new initiative, the world has changed, and it is time to launch yet another.

But strangulation by complexity is not an inevitable fate. Perhaps the most important contribution of this book is that it explains the consistent way that enduringly successful companies maintain a form of simplicity at their core. They have done so by creating what we call *Great Repeatable Models* that adhere to a consistent set of principles. We hope you enjoy and benefit from this journey of discovery.

To learn more about the ideas in this book, visit www.repeat ability.com.

The Great Repeatable Model

What do a tiffin tin, a Billy bookcase, and Michael Jordan have in common?

Each is central to a business success story that transformed its market. Each is emblematic of a company that learned to replicate and adapt its early successes over and over, often for decades, in a world of constant change.

It is an uncommon message, perhaps, in a world so dominated by change, where siren-like voices of gurus, analysts, and pundits preach "reinvention" on the part of companies. We find the opposite. Our data shows that simplicity, focus, and mastering the art of continuous change nearly always trump strategies of radical change or constant reinvention. The complexity and disruption that result are the great "silent killers" of growth and can even lead to "binge and purge" cycles that ultimately weaken the core of businesses.

We find in our research that enduring success is not about the choice of market, but about the essential design of a company (a much more controllable variable) and about harnessing the power of continuous improvement and adaptation—driving learning and competitive advantage deeper and deeper into the fabric of a business. This book is dedicated to pinpointing the essential nature of those companies in tough and dynamic competitive arenas that have been able to change continuously in order to repeat their successes again and again. We call them the *Great Repeatable Models*.

Let us illustrate with three quick examples and then begin our journey in search of the secrets of the Great Repeatable Models.

The Dabbawallas of Mumbai

Visitors to Mumbai can be easily overwhelmed by the scale and pace of India's most densely populated city. Yet every day, amid the noise, traffic, and bustle, the five thousand *dabbawallas* of the Nutan Mumbai Tiffin Box Suppliers' Charity Trust deliver two hundred thousand boxed lunches, cooked the same morning in people's homes or by special caterers, to the right people on time. At night, the system reverses, and the dabbawallas return the color-coded lunch boxes—called *dabbas*—to where they came from. The average box travels 60 kilometers on bikes, on trains, on pushcarts, and on foot and is handled by six different people.

Despite the complexity of this supply chain, the dabbawallas perform so well that the odds of delivering the wrong lunch to a customer are less than one in 6 million, a statistic that has drawn attention from operations specialists across the world and that conforms to Six Sigma quality levels. The distinctive deliverymen, dressed in white cotton uniforms and white caps, pride themselves on making deliveries in the severest conditions.

The service ethos is so strong, in fact, that when Britain's Prince Charles asked whether he could meet some dabbawallas, they insisted he schedule the meeting between delivery cycles.

The association would look little changed to a time traveler from the 1890s, when Mahadeo Havaji Bacche founded it. The service ethos has certainly been there from the start. The lunch boxes and uniforms are largely the same. The bicycles, trains, and pushcarts haven't changed a lot either. But the barefoot dabbawallas don't ignore the march of progress; they have always been ready to take advantage of innovations. Today they all carry mobile phones and use them to coordinate deliveries and alert each other to problems. Orders are now taken on the Internet and by text messaging. The trust even tracks customer satisfaction levels through online customer polling. This careful blend of the old and the new has translated into enduring success. In the nearly 125 years since its creation, the association has become a constant fixture in Mumbai's food delivery business and is growing profitably at between 5 percent and 10 percent a year. It is a simple example of a repeatable success formula that has had to constantly adapt to change, but has driven the art of continuous improvement in its core to a high level. The combination has repelled every competitor in sight for over a century.

IKEA and the Billy Bookcase

From its iconic blue-and-yellow stores to its ubiquitous customer-assembled Billy bookcase, IKEA is one of the most recognizable and admired companies in the world. It turns over 23 billion euros from 626 million visitors to its 280 stores in more than 25 countries. In Europe, it is at least 12 times as large as its nearest competitor.

The core features of this hugely successful company have changed only incrementally since Ingvar Kamprad opened the first IKEA furniture stores in Sweden during the 1950s. Since those early years, all wooden furniture sold in the stores has been sold in flat packs for self-assembly by the customer, all stores have been built around a flow that encourages cross-selling, all products have been designed to hit a target selling price, and the company has carefully maintained an extremely egalitarian corporate culture. IKEA has not attempted to diversify into businesses that would require a different model, nor has it ever reinvented itself.

Instead, it has focused on maintaining those differentiations, making its economics more efficient and improving product design, on the one hand, and, on the other hand, carefully selecting new product categories and geographies where the model can work. Its ability to do this is based on the fact that everyone in the company has internalized a long-held set of relatively simple, transparent rules and principles—so all decisions in the organization across all levels of employees tend to reinforce and improve the model. IKEA, therefore, is not a story of a search for hot markets—furniture has been around for a long time—it is a story of the development of a hot business model.

Some might view IKEA as a bit retro in a world of constant change—furniture, retail, low technology. Yet, the truth is that this is a market with an enormous number of new entrants in each region of the world, lots of technology in supply chain and materials, new Internet sales models, and constant change in consumer needs. The IKEA repeatable model—as with the dabbawallas—has adapted and endured and constantly learned and improved, while others have failed to do so. The business has mastered the art of continual change and continual improvement.

The Swoosh of NIKE

NIKE, Inc. defines athletic innovation, speed, and constant change. It is one of the cases that started us on our path to repeatable models. In twenty-five years, from 1986 to 2011, NIKE, Inc. has grown from less than a billion dollars in size to nearly $21 billion, with EBIT of $2.8 billion. NIKE has averaged a 20 percent annual total return to shareholders over the entire twenty-five-year period. If you had invested $100 in NIKE in 1984, it would be worth more than $10,000 today. Not bad performance in a market that is time and time again defined as low growth and commodity-based.

NIKE's repeatable model is built on four core interlocking capabilities: (1) brand management (the ubiquitous swoosh), (2) athlete partnerships, (3) award-winning design and use of new materials, and (4) an efficient supply chain to Asia (it owns no manufacturing assets). In 1989, NIKE and its main rival, Reebok, were comparable in size, product line, brand recognition, and profitability. Yet, Reebok never found a repeatable formula—careening from Ralph Lauren footwear to Boston Whaler boats, to Western boots, to golf clothing. As a result, Reebok did not create a learning organization as it jumped from one *idée du jour* to another, and it created virtually no economic value in the stock market for two decades until it was sold in 2006 to Adidas. Meanwhile, NIKE posted a record-setting performance, redefined the rules of the game of its industry, and reshaped and enlarged the global profit pool that supports it.

What is especially interesting about the NIKE example is the direct head-to-head comparison with a rival. Reports at the time were referring to the pair with phrases like "Coke vs. Pepsi," "in an intense race for America's footwear," "neck and neck," and so on. Yet, the repeatable model of NIKE, and its relentless ability to innovate and improve year after year, prevailed over one that was not so, while fending off new challengers in a dynamic market that has seen monumental changes in the economics of sports, dramatic shifts in media, channel evolution, and the Internet, and the advent of new materials technology and supply chain patterns.

Three companies on three continents in three very different markets. Each—furniture, athletic shoes, food delivery—looks like a commodity on the surface, yet a closer look shows that each actually has had enormous change to deal with on many dimensions, from customer needs to channel shifts to technology to the Internet. Yet, each has managed to adapt, to continuously improve, and to fend off a constantly changing onslaught of competitors. On the surface, businesses like IKEA do not look that mysterious, but no competitor has come close. Only IKEA, it seems, knows how to imitate IKEA.

On the face of it, this is a paradox. Yet, as you read through this book you will come to recognize, like us, that long-term success actually requires a foundation of enduring and stable core principles. Without the stabilizing effect of a set of core strategic and organizational principles, companies can fall prey to a form of "corporate ADD" (attention deficit disorder) that dooms them to cycles of destruction and reinvention and the endless search for the hot market that will propel them miraculously to a better world. In their quest for some kind of silver bullet, many companies have not built up the muscles of constant improvement and focus. The extremes of such behavior are not that common—how could they be?—but the more subtle and pernicious versions of it are everywhere.

During the course of this book, you will encounter companies that took the road less traveled and created Great Repeatable Models to achieve sustained performance in a wide range of circumstances. Some, like NIKE, IKEA, Tetra Pak, and Olam, have been developing and refining their Great Repeatable Model from the very beginning. Others, like LEGO, are classic cases of management teams that prematurely abandoned their repeatable model, only to discover that their best hope was to return to it with new vigor and renewal. And still others, like DaVita, used these ideas to take a near-bankrupt company, yet one with strong underlying assets and a history of a repeatable model, and renew its growth and vitality.

Let's begin with the research.

The Search for Profitable Growth

Sustained and profitable growth is rare and becoming increasingly so. A decade ago, we found that only about 13 percent of companies in the world had achieved, on average, even a modest rate of profitable growth (5.5 percent in real terms) over the decade while also earning their cost of capital. In the last decade, ending in 2010, the percentage had dropped to only 9 percent—this despite the fact that well over 90 percent of companies aspire to this level of performance in their strategic plans.

Our work on repeatable models caps a ten-year project that we have undertaken at Bain & Company on the changing origins of profitable growth and the methods for capturing it. We are finding that it is much less about the choice of hot market than about the how and the why of strategy and the business model that translates it into action. Moreover, we find that strategy is becoming less and less about a rigid plan to pursue growth markets than about developing a general direction built around deep and uniquely strong capabilities that constantly learn, continuously improve, test, and adjust in manageable increments to the changing market (as opposed to hesitancy followed by an anxious rush to make up for lost time).

We have used a rich set of data in the course of this research, including:

- A database of 8,000 global companies over 25 years, used to look at the relationship of patterns of strategy to results, and to identify the best long-term performers

- A database of 200 companies, with characteristics of practices, business models, and performance

- Thirty case examples, including many executive interviews

- A global survey of 377 executives conducted with the Economist Intelligence Unit[1]

- Focused analysis of groups of high performers—superfast growers, very long-term sustained and profitable companies, the oldest companies, and the most innovative companies

- Examination of the architecture of repeatable models in other fields, from biology to history, to the design of the Internet

That research effort has already produced a large body of work on how companies find their next wave of profitable growth, reported in numerous articles and three prior books with Harvard Business Review Press. Three "golden threads" from that work form the intellectual underpinning of this book:

- *It is more about the company.* We find over and over that 80 percent of variation in financial returns among all businesses in the world is accounted for by their performance relative to other companies within their industry, as opposed to their choice of market. Market power and influence through a strongly differentiated strategy, what we call *leadership economics*, is the greatest single explainer of relative business performance. Our book *Profit from the Core* documented through hundreds of case examples how easy it is for businesses to lose strategic focus, fail to see the full potential of their existing assets and capabilities, and prematurely abandon their core (and later regret it).[2]

- *Most new growth initiatives fail.* We find that new growth initiatives—organic or by acquisition—have success rates of only about 20–25 percent, much lower than most executives realize. Moreover, most managers say, in retrospect, that their growth initiatives proved to be more complex than they had expected and often had negative impacts on the growth of the "core of the core" business itself. We found this phenomenon, which we call the *trap of false enthusiasm*, in hundreds of examples—from Bausch & Lomb to Citigroup (merged with Travelers) to Daimler-Benz (entering aerospace and later buying Chrysler, both disasters that weakened the core) and on and on. Our book *Beyond the Core* showed how the odds of success can be influenced through a more systematic approach to making growth investments, as a portfolio of bets, and to the decoding of lessons from past experiences in terms of what worked and what failed.[3] The odds of success depend critically on whether the idea involves current customers, on the economic distance of the idea from the company's core, on whether the idea is part of a repeatable model, and on whether the core platform has achieved leadership economics in its primary market.

- *Redefinition rarely works.* We found that many businesses evolved over time through a cycle of core focus, adjacency expansion from the core (ideally with a repeatable model), and inevitable crisis leading to redefinition. We called this the focus-expand-redefine cycle of growth. The odds of success (surviving and reestablishing a profitable trajectory) in redefinition are extremely low, less than one in ten. The exceptions— such as Marvel Entertainment (from comics to movies), IBM (from hardware to services and software), and De Beers (from mining to consumer focus and retail)— were able to rebuild their core model around "hidden assets," deep strengths in the core business that had not been previously utilized. This was the focus of our book *Unstoppable*.[4] The work on repeatable models reported on in this book has the potential, we believe, to allow companies to learn and adapt sooner, faster, and in smaller increments, reducing both the potential for a crisis of redefinition and the entropy of building around a nonrepeatable model, from which few emerge as real champions.

These three findings are still as true as ever. Now we introduce another strand that pulls it all together—a how-to of business model design built around a few principles that harness the power of repeatability. A *business model* is defined usually as a blueprint that translates strategy into key decisions and actions, where the pieces are evident and self-reinforcing—a sort of virtuous cycle.[5] We feel it necessary to revise this view because a business model that is to endure in the dynamic markets of today must integrate strategy, deep core principles, and cultural norms with a survival mechanism to constantly improve and adapt the model (while still running the business and delivering results). This is the focus of this book—the strategic architecture of the most lasting business success stories.

Lessons from Businesses with Enduring Success

Sustained success in a world of more rapid change is not easy. It requires the simultaneous ability to focus and improve your deepest strengths of the past while at the same time adapting your business and adding new capabilities for the future. Within the world of science, you find that the most enduring and adaptive systems, from genetics to the design of the Internet, have a set of common architectural principles at their core that help to achieve this balance of focus and adaptation. When we studied the most enduring and adaptable businesses, we found the same thing.

One elite group we called "rocket ships." These were notable for the *speed* of their profitable growth, from a low base to more than $10 billion within twenty years, consistently delivering more than 15 percent annual return to shareholders. In the seven public stock exchanges in our database (which excluded financial service and natural resource companies), we identified thirty-one rocket ships, which we rated on a number of dimensions, such as the strength of their core, their method of growth, and the existence of a well-documented repeatable model as expressed by the analysts who follow the companies, by business writers, and by the companies' reports. We found that 90 percent of these super-high-performing rocket ships employed a clear repeatable model that propelled their growth strategy. The majority of these grew primarily through organic means—such as Amazon, Google, and NIKE. Though the data was not always comparable, when we extended the analysis to companies in the developing world, like Huawei, Hankook Tire, Larsen & Toubro, or Nine Dragons Paper, we found the same thing. Less than half used acquisition as an additional means to achieve growth and add capabilities—such as Danaher, Medtronic, and EMC.

A second elite group that we studied consisted of long-term sustained performers. We defined these by their ability to grow sustainably (5.5 percent real growth) and profitably (earning their cost of capital) for two decades. We found that three-fourths of these elite performers grew from a single primary core business replicating an easily recognizable model. About half of them participated in naturally repeatable industries like retail (e.g., Wal-Mart, Target, Lowe's, Best Buy, Tesco, and Walgreens), in which opportunities for replicating a business model are fairly intuitive. But there were also many companies that were able to replicate and adapt their initial business models across less obvious contexts, such as the distributor Sysco, the logistics company Expeditors, the medical technologies company Medtronic, or the iconic motorcycle company Harley-Davidson.

We extended this examination of long-term performers to the best performers at innovation by considering the top twenty companies on *BusinessWeek*'s Most Innovative Companies 2009 list. We found that over 60 percent of these Companies scored high on our rating of their repeatable models (average of 4 or above on a scale of 5). In fact, many of the companies on this list emphasize their repeatable model for innovation, such as Procter & Gamble's (P&G) Connect+Develop program to pursue its goal that half of major new product ideas originate outside the company, and Apple with its methodical approach to launching new, innovative products.

Finally, we examined the oldest surviving companies in the world to understand the root causes of their unusual and extreme ability to prosper over centuries. For instance, the oldest currently active business is a Japanese lodging business called Hoshi Ryokan, which has focused on its core of inns in Japan since its founding in 718. Hoshi Ryokan is now managed by the forty-sixth generation of the Hoshi family, using many principles of hospitality established by its founders. Most of the businesses we examined with the longest continuous lives stayed entirely focused on a specific niche that had evolved gradually since the company's founding around a relatively simple original model. The power of such long-standing companies, constantly refining their repeatable formula in a focused single market or niche, can be especially seen in the so-called hidden champions identified and celebrated in a book by Hermann Simon. Such focused, single-core companies, often family businesses with long histories (83 percent were over twenty-five years old and 31 percent were over seventy-five years old), are credited with being the key source of stability of the German economy that gave it such strength and resilience during the recent global financial crisis.[6]

For instance, take Faber-Castell, the world leader in pencils since its founding in 1761 in Stein, Germany. Today, the company produces more than 2.2 billion pencils per year and has led a market that has grown for centuries. Indeed, even during the recent recession, the revenues of Faber-Castell increased by 6 percent.[7] The company's first major innovation (other than figuring out how to put lead inside a wooden tube in its initial incarnation) was the hexagonal pencil that would not roll off desks. Subsequent innovations included new colors, forms of pencils with superior environmental properties, and even tiny rubber bumps on the outside of pencils making them easier to grip in hot climates. It is repeatability through eight generations of a family business.

Given our new findings that repeatable models were central to more than three-quarters of the cases of sustained profitable growth, we set out to discover what features of a repeatable business model actually matter the most and what insights can be used most readily by businesses to improve.

New Finding: How Repeatability Drives Success

The starting place for us in our pursuit of the design principles of the Great Repeatable Models was a database of two hundred companies that we created to examine thirty different factors that had emerged from our case examples of Great Repeatable Models and interviews with executives in those businesses. What we found surprised us. We were able to explain 40–50 percent of performance variation within an industry just from the ratings regarding adherence to three sets of design principles. This is a remarkable level of explanatory power, given the number of other variables that we considered like choice of market, scale, whether the company was diversified or not, whether growth was organic or not, and the nature of the key metrics that they focus on.

Principle 1: A Strong, Well-Differentiated Core

Differentiation is the essence of strategy, the root cause of competitive advantage, and a major driver of relative profitability among businesses. You earn money in business by being different from competitors—in a way that gives you superiority in serving your core customers or superior cost economics that lets you outinvest your competitors—not just from performing a valuable task. The Great Repeatable Models were sharply, almost obviously, differentiated relative to competitors along a dimension that also allowed for differential profitability. The unique assets, deep competencies, and capabilities that make this differentiation possible and that are translated into behaviors and product features define the "core of the core" of the business. These are the crown jewels. At their best, these core activities (such as character development at Pixar, or risk management and arbitrage in agricultural commodities at Olam, or flat package furniture design at IKEA, or the Toyota Production System) drive learning, constant change, and improvement, and they increase further barriers to imitation.

Principle 2: Clear Nonnegotiables

An important factor in success was a common understanding on the part of management and employees of the company's core values and the key criteria used to make trade-offs in decision making. We call these principles, used to translate strategy into consistent decisions and actions, the *nonnegotiables*. Clear nonnegotiables improve the focus and simplicity of strategy by translating it into practical behavioral rules and prohibitions. This, in turn, has the effect of reducing the distance from management to the front line (and back). Our data shows that today relatively few businesses can claim these attributes.[8]

Improving the translation of strategy to behaviors and mindset is a major improvement opportunity for many companies. Our research at Bain shows that the main driver of employee loyalty and commitment is a belief in the values of the management team and the organization's strategy. It is tough to mobilize around a change if everyone sees the world totally differently, does not understand the strategy, and does not have shared vocabulary and priorities. Yet, as the data we explore later in chapter 3 suggests, most businesses that grow over time become encumbered by layers of complexity that widen this gap, reduce customer responsiveness, and create diseconomies of scale. Think of this the next time you get lost in an infinite phone menu as you try to get advice on how to use your mobile phone, fix problems with your computer, or discuss a concern with an airline representative.

Principle 3: Systems for closed-loop learning

The Great Repeatable Models exhibited more self-conscious methods than their competitors, on average, to perceive and try to adapt to change. They especially tended to have well-developed systems to learn and drive continuous improvement across the business, leveraging the transparency and consistency of their repeatable model. The methods we describe later—of how Apple and LEGO and Vanguard stay in touch with their customers or how Toyota and Danaher and AB InBev stay in touch with frontline production experience—are examples.

The second form of closed-loop learning relates to those less frequent situations when fundamental change in the marketplace (like a new technology, competitor model, or customer need) threatens a key premise of the repeatable model itself. A company's inability to adapt or to have a sufficient sense of urgency in response to a potentially mortal threat has resulted in the stall-out of some of the great successes in business. Consider, for instance, Kodak confronting digital technology, Nokia confronting smart phones, traditional airlines confronting low-cost carriers, IBM confronting the PC, Xerox confronting printers and low-cost entrants, and newspapers dealing with the shift of media online. This is the phenomenon of *disruptive innovation*, well described by Clayton Christensen in his book *The Innovator's Dilemma*, which often emerges in the bottom of the market or in neglected segments and spreads almost inexorably, disrupting incumbents who underreact to the threat.[9]

To respond to this challenge, many businesses have redesigned part of their strategy development in order to strengthen the forms of feedback and the way the loop is closed. For example, in IBM's case, the redesign was perhaps a reaction to its prior crisis, which was born of slow reaction to the emergence of the personal computer. Huawei, the rapidly growing Chinese challenger to network equipment incumbents such as Ericsson and Alcatel-Lucent, has a permanent office of restructuring, which reports to the chairman and is focused exactly on identifying external threats to its model and pushing for a strong response.

These are the three design principles that emerged from our research. We found strong empirical evidence of their importance in explaining sustained performance over time and relative performance versus other businesses. The data from our two hundred–company study, to which we return throughout this book, is summarized in figure 1-1. The figure shows a

FIGURE 1-1

Scores on design principles by performance group

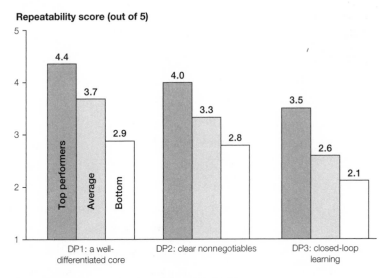

Repeatability score (out of 5)

Source: Bain 200 Company Database of Repeatable Models.

highly statistically significant difference in the three clusters of practices that we studied across these companies, when the companies were grouped by financial performance. The lowest average ratings and the widest differences across companies were in the area of clear systems to react to feedback and adapt.

These empirical results show the links among the three design principles and business performance. Few businesses that were rated below 3.5 (on a scale of 1 to 5) on all three design principles performed at a high level. By contrast, 70 percent of the companies that were rated at 3.5 and above for all three design principles at the same time outperformed.

The results are so central to the premise of this book—that the Great Repeatable Models are based on three design principles—that we did a further validation. We worked with the Economist Intelligence Unit in March 2011 to survey 377 executives across the world in 377 different companies.[10] We asked them about the relative performance of their companies and about their perceptions with regard to the practices that underpin our three design principles. We found almost identical results to those of the two hundred–company database derived from a completely different method. For instance, when we looked at which companies were rated 4 or 5 on the 1-to-5 scale regarding the existence of a well-differentiated core and a supporting activity system, we found a 2.7 times difference versus bottom performers (77 percent versus 29 percent). For questions regarding core principles and clear nonnegotiables, the difference was 2.2 times (74 percent versus 33 percent). And for questions regarding learning and feedback systems, the difference was 6.1 times (though lower for all, 61 percent versus 10 percent).

The design principles were mutually reinforcing. Businesses that adhered to one design principle usually adhered to others. For instance, businesses seen to have a clear repeatable differentiation had a 64 percent chance of adhering strongly to one of the other two design principles.

How Great Repeatable Models Succeed

In our experience, the virtuous, reinforcing cycle found in the Great Repeatable Models among the three design principles usually works like this (see figure 1-2). A clear, repeatable differentiation (design principle 1) makes common measures and beliefs easier to create and use (design principle 2), which drives more transparency, learning, and adaptation (design principle 3), which in turn pushes the entire business down an experience curve faster than less repeatable competitors.

FIGURE 1-2

The design principles of Great Repeatable Models

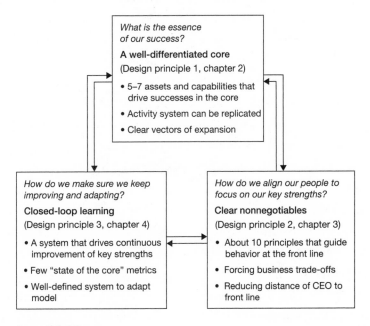

What is the essence of our success?

A well-differentiated core
(Design principle 1, chapter 2)

- 5–7 assets and capabilities that drive successes in the core
- Activity system can be replicated
- Clear vectors of expansion

How do we make sure we keep improving and adapting?

Closed-loop learning
(Design principle 3, chapter 4)

- A system that drives continuous improvement of key strengths
- Few "state of the core" metrics
- Well-defined system to adapt model

How do we align our people to focus on our key strengths?

Clear nonnegotiables
(Design principle 2, chapter 3)

- About 10 principles that guide behavior at the front line
- Forcing business trade-offs
- Reducing distance of CEO to front line

Source: Bain & Company.

The mutual fund company Vanguard is a great example of the virtuous dynamic. Vanguard was founded by John Bogle in 1974 with eleven managed mutual funds and $1.8 billion in assets. But Bogle believed passionately in the proposition that no actively managed fund could outperform the market in the long run. Why, therefore, should investors pay a fee for active management? He developed an alternative: passive funds that simply tracked market indexes. They would need no fund managers or researchers and could therefore charge fees considerably lower than the actively managed alternatives. Instead of providing what he saw as essentially useless stock-picking advice, Bogle felt he should offer customers responsive service and advice on the types or classes of investments that would be suitable for investors' needs. When this form of fund was first offered as Index Trust in 1976 it was derided by the popular business press. Yet the idea took hold and became the mainstay of Vanguard and its core differentiation of low-cost investing, of which index funds represented the purest form of that idea.

Vanguard has remained true to this simple, stark differentiation ever since, a strategy that has paid off handsomely. In 2009, in the depths of the financial crisis, Vanguard became the largest mutual fund company in the world, with $1.6 trillion of assets under management (capturing an amazing 45 percent of the new money coming into the market that year). Of course, it has diversified over the years into new forms of indexed funds and new customer segments. Yet, despite its larger size, Vanguard never has strayed from its core principles of low-cost investing, long-term customer loyalty (its churn rate is one-third that of the industry), employee egalitarianism, and conservative investing, all combined in a repeatable business model.

Now let's look at the second feature. The company is named for HMS *Vanguard*, a seventy-four-gun ship of Admiral Horatio Nelson, one of the greatest strategists in naval warfare. Nelson's battles were fought generally by the rules of the day—conventional line-of-battle approach, training in close-order combat, and signaling systems among ships. However, the line of battle typically extended beyond the horizon of sight. During the confusion and smoke of battle, and the destruction of masts, communication became worse than unreliable. Nelson's solution to this problem was to spend so much time training his crews that each boat became a repeatable replica of his thinking and behaviors. In fact, he met with them so frequently that he named them his "band of brothers." As a result, he could trust his subordinates to act as he would, rather than relying on cumbersome command and control tactics. Though they appeared to be separate, they were perceived as acting in an uncannily coordinated way, as a single mind, more than their adversaries had ever seen, resulting in victories with many fewer casualties over and over again against larger French fleets.

Bogle's imitation of Nelson went beyond the name. He called employees "crewmembers," and he laid the foundations for a distinctive egalitarian culture, strongly rooted in the company's differentiated value proposition. The company's activities and decisions are all guided by a set of statements called "Simple Truths" that are remarkably consistent with the initial conception of the business, though they have been added to and embellished over the years. They include the following:

- Most investors cannot "beat the market" long term.

- The best customers are loyal, long-term investors.

- We do not pay for distribution of our products.

- Low expense ratios drive high returns.

- A mutual organization owned by the "funds" is best for investors.

- Egalitarianism must define how we work together.

What Repeatable Models Are *Not*

It is worth taking a moment to reflect on what we do *not* mean by a repeatable model, for the word *repeatable* can have many connotations beyond the idea of repeating your greatest successes systematically. Here are a few things that a Great Repeatable Model is not:

- It is *not* the performance of a repetitive task like a robot. We are talking about the essence of a business requiring constant judgment, but needing some consistency in order to drive learning.

- It is *not* the mechanical replication everywhere of a business concept. Our focus is where and how to modify a concept so that it can repeat its greatest successes and adapt to new conditions. Indeed, many of the best Great Repeatable Models were not in "naturally repeatable" businesses, but often were companies that brought a new level of clarity and

The distinctive features of Vanguard's business model reinforce each other; its management even uses a diagram of a self-reinforcing cycle to describe the company's strategy (see figure 1-3). Vanguard's strong differentiation and leadership in the area of indexed funds (mutual funds constructed to track the averages) both inform and are driven by its investment philosophy. Similarly, Vanguard's low-cost position (its expenses charged to customers are one-sixth those of its competitors) is reinforced by its belief in not paying for distribution and its commitment to a mutual structure in which profits are shared with the investors. Finally, Vanguard's heavy investment in its telephone representatives and customer advisers discipline—as IKEA did—to a market that was messy and undisciplined.

- It is *not* an endless to-do list handed down to every frontline employee. That form of repeatability suppresses feedback and is demotivating and soulless. Our search is for repeatability that creates freedom, but within a framework.

- It is *not* the repeatability of nonstrategic functions. Every company has critical functions in finance, tax, real estate, and on and on. These are essential enablers, but we are focused on the handful of differentiators that really drive competitive advantage. This is the essence of strategy today.

We could list many other things that repeatable models are not meant to be, including boring, demotivating, mindless, or overly mechanical. These trade-offs and tensions are at the center of why it is so hard to do it well, yet so powerful and differentiating when you get it right.

not only reinforces the core beliefs in loyalty and the key role of employees as the customers' interface with Vanguard, but also enables the company to obtain direct customer feedback in ways that competitors without the same frontline service investment have trouble matching.

Reflecting on the company's stellar performance, CEO Bill McNabb told us, "The secret to our success is how we have managed our repeatable model to get better and better every year, while still adapting and adhering to the deep business principles that were set in place at the time of John Bogle. This discipline has not only led us in the right direction, but often prevented us from going astray."[11]

FIGURE 1-3

Vanguard's self-reinforcing cycle, with examples of practices driving the strategy

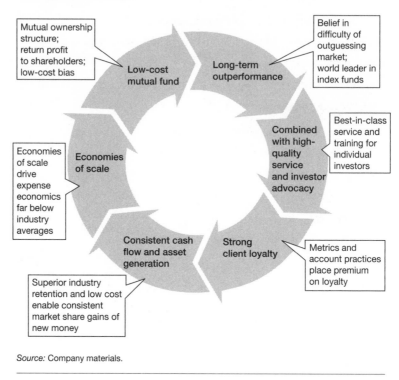

Mutual ownership structure; return profit to shareholders; low-cost bias

Belief in difficulty of outguessing market; world leader in index funds

Low-cost mutual fund

Long-term outperformance

Best-in-class service and training for individual investors

Combined with high-quality service and investor advocacy

Economies of scale drive expense economics far below industry averages

Economies of scale

Consistent cash flow and asset generation

Strong client loyalty

Metrics and account practices place premium on loyalty

Superior industry retention and low cost enable consistent market share gains of new money

Source: Company materials.

The power of repeatable models can also be seen as a key motivator behind a number of major M&A deals. Take the case of Pixar, which the Walt Disney Company bought for $7.4 billion in 2006, despite the fact that it had produced only six movies and accumulated revenues of only $3.2 billion, less than half of the purchase price. What Pixar had (and still has) was a remarkable model for producing animated movies. Eleven straight releases were number one at the box office in their first week—a Hollywood record—and Pixar won seven Oscars between 2003 and 2010 for best animated movie. *Toy Story 3*, released in 2010, is the most profitable animated film of all time. Pixar's is a repeatable model that may ultimately transform the whole of Disney's movie business.

There's More Than One Formula

When you read about companies with Great Repeatable Models like IKEA and Vanguard, it's tempting to conclude that somehow the company has come up with a dominant business model. In a sense, this is true. A Great Repeatable Model will dominate non-Great non-Repeatable Models. But that doesn't mean that there's only one possible Great Repeatable Model in an industry. Our research of the high performers shows that in fact there are multiple Great Repeatable Models in almost any industry, even in highly competitive, mature ones—which reinforces our finding that performance is more about managerial decisions than the business you happen to be in.

Take the airline business, arguably the toughest way to make money. In the ten years from 2000 to 2010, the airline industry destroyed more than $200 billion in shareholder value. During this period, 90 percent of the top one hundred global airlines did not even earn their cost of capital, scant reward for the valuable service that each performs. Forty-eight bankruptcies in the United States (including United, Pan Am, TWA, US Airways, and Delta) were filed in the same period. Yet, amid all this horrible news, two very successful airlines have created very different Great Repeatable Models.

One of these is the low-cost carrier Ryanair, whose stock price increased more than threefold in the decade from 2000 to 2010, not a great period for the airline industry in general. Its Great Repeatable Model is about stripping the airline experience and cost model down to its absolute basics. The company was one of the first to charge for checked bags and was a pioneer in online check-in, which is now mandatory for all passengers. This value proposition is deeply internalized. As CEO Michael O'Leary puts it, "We're open about our policies: You're not getting free food. We don't want your check-in bags. We're not going to put you up in hotels because your granny died. But we are going to guarantee you the lowest airfares in Europe, by a distance . . . And that's what people really want—affordable, safe air transport from A to B. It's a commodity. It's not some life changing sexual experience, which is what the other high-fare airlines have tried to convince you it is."[12]

The model of Ryanair differs sharply from that of Singapore Airlines (SIA), whose financial performance is about its only point of similarity with Ryanair. SIA has been profitable every year since its founding in 1972 and has won the Readers' Choice Award for Global Airlines from *Condé Nast Traveler* an astonishing twenty-two of twenty-three times by offering passengers just the type of service that O'Leary derides. It is able to do this, however, because its organizational qualities relative to the competition's have made it an extremely cost-effective operator. One detailed study of SIA's economics concluded, "It's intriguing that SIA has combined the supposedly incompatible strategies of differentiation—which it pursues through service excellence and continuous innovation—and cost leadership. Few firms have executed a dual strategy profitably . . . the dual strategy has become part of the airline's organizational DNA over the years."[13] Differentiation? Organizational DNA? To us they sound like elements of a Great Repeatable Model, one that's very different from Ryanair's.

How Repeatable Models Stop Repeating

We believe after years of study that the underlying principles of the Great Repeatable Models provide the best recipe for creating a lasting competitive advantage. However, every strong idea brings with it some potential vulnerabilities that must be recognized and guarded against. Consider the following.

Dell, Nokia, and Starbucks are three iconic businesses fueled by some of the Great Repeatable Models of the past twenty-five years. Dell was the top-performing large global firm of the 1990s. Nokia captured more than 90 percent of the profit pool of the global handset market through most of the 1990s, decimating a series of tough competitors from Samsung to Motorola. From the early 1990s through 2006, Starbucks' stock price grew by more than fifty times as it opened twelve thousand stores and became the company in the world with the largest number of different customers encountered every day. Each company was a model of focus and a paradigm of repeatability. Yet, all stalled out for different reasons that a highly successful repeatable model could be prone to.

Two prominent reasons why once seemingly invincible business models lost momentum are loss of focus on the core and failure to adapt rapidly enough.

The most common reason is *loss of focus*, often accompanied by an erosion of operational excellence in the core and an increase in entropy or a sense of heightened disorder at the front line of the core business. Some version of this syndrome of distraction characterized about two-thirds of the cases of stall-out of repeatable models that we examined. In none of these cases was the stall-out due to the inherent invalidity of the model or the disappearance of the more fundamental customer need it was trying to fulfill—quite the opposite.

For instance, from 2007 to 2009, Starbucks saw its market value decline by more than 70 percent, including a drop of 42 percent in 2007 alone. Its founder, Howard Schultz, returned as CEO, and the company closed seven hundred stores and undertook a major effort to return to its coffee core. On his return, Schultz wrote a memo to his management team saying that uncontrolled growth of the model had caused a "series of decisions that, in retrospect, have led to the watering down of the Starbucks Experience, and what some might call the commoditization of our brand."[14] He highlighted the company's movements into movies, music, forms of cooked food in the store (melted cheese) that contaminated the distinctive coffee aroma, and on and on. He set about to reverse this trend, rejuvenating the repeatable model of the past, returning the value of the company close to its historic high. The problem was not the model, but how it was being implemented and no longer constantly improved, and how its consistent success created the opportunity for distraction. This was a common pattern—boredom, neglect, loss of focus, but ultimate return to a next generation version of the core formula—seen in a range of stories of corporate renewal cited throughout our research, from Procter & Gamble to LEGO to Hilti.

The second key reason that successful, repeatable models hit the wall is *failure to adapt fast enough* as changing markets and technologies weaken the original source of competitive advantage that propelled the company in earlier years. This characterized about 30 percent of the cases of stall-out or decline that we examined. The reversal of fortune for Dell and the flattening of its stock price from 2000 through 2008 was the result of the customer, cost, and product advantages of its unique direct model (tailored PCs, near-zero inventory, 12–15 percent cost advantage, direct customer contact) gradually narrowing versus competitors. Dell is now reinvigorating its business model and playing catch-up in adaptation. Recent earnings and stock price results are showing positive early signs of renewal. This is an easy trap to fall into for a company with a fantastically successful formula, and it is the reason why our third design principle emphasizes highly visible, objective, and strong feedback processes with clear links to decision making.

Often the changes in the marketplace that companies face are incremental, as was the case with Dell. Sometimes, however, a true paradigm shift occurs in an industry, often built around a new technology, that threatens to render obsolete some or all of an incumbent's repeatable model. Despite this being the case in a relatively small percentage of models that lost momentum, it receives much press, perhaps because it creates newsworthy crises in its aftermath.

Clayton Christensen has extensively described and studied disruptive innovation of this sort. It can take the form of a new market segment emerging at the top of the market or a low-cost model that first attacked the segments of lower interest to the leader, sort of flying under the radar. An example of the former is Nokia and the threat to its handset business from the emergence of smart phones. An example of the latter is the newspaper business, as with the *New York Times* confronting the challenge of free and instant information over the Internet. Both are disruptive innovations that threatened the heart of a once dominant form of repeatable model. Take Nokia, for instance, to see how this could happen.

Nokia is the world's leading mobile handset manufac-turer and at one point, the sixth most valuable brand in the world. A true national treasure of Finland, it has accounted for 1.6 percent of the country's gross domestic product. In the mid-1990s, Nokia captured more than 40 percent of the global market share of mobile phone units and, by our estimates, more than 80 percent of the profit pool. It took on dozens of compet-itors over this time and won handily. The closest one, Samsung, achieved market share only one-third that of Nokia. Nokia's business model defined the gold standard for a repeatable model. The form factors and manufacturing configurations were repeatable across models and years, driving enormous scale. Its world-class supply chain system made it the number one firm in the world in an independent study of supply chain management in 2007. Business schools and management teams everywhere studied the brilliance of its accomplishments.

During the era of the first-generation mobile handsets, Nokia would score off the charts on most of our design principles. It was differentiated on cost, reliability, and the breadth of its channels. It had strong core principles and beliefs that pervaded the company and created a powerful culture. And it had systems for short-term product adaptation to customers and to suppliers. For instance, in India, starting in 2006, the Nokia handset designed through detailed work in rural areas (water resistant to monsoons, stronger light for blackouts, Hindi language, etc.) captured about 70 percent of market share—a successful example of short-term adaptability.

On top of this, Nokia had not only the incentives to invest to protect its core model, but also the resources. The company was so awash in cash (for instance, more than 9 billion euros on the balance sheet in cash in 2002, just before smart phone developments emerged) that it was paying out 30–40 percent of profits in large dividends and buying its stock back aggressively—not always a great sign for a technology-centered company facing an existential challenge from new technology; this concerned analysts who followed the company.

By 2010, Nokia had grown to be a company with nearly 43 billion euros in revenues, and with almost 2 billion euros of pretax profit. But it was in crisis. Though the business still held more than 32 percent of global market share, its share of the profit pool was dropping like a stone. Yet, by June 2010, just a few months before the board moved to replace Nokia's CEO and others on the team, Apple had sold $21 billion worth of iPhones and applications, according to the *International Herald Tribune*. That was about half as much as Nokia sold worldwide of all its forms of mobile phones.

"Stifling bureaucracy led to lack of action on early smart phone innovation," the *Herald Tribune* headlined its well-reported article. The article continued: "A few years before Apple introduced the iPhone in early 2007, the prototype of an Internet ready, touch screen handset with a large display made the rounds among upper management at Nokia. The prototype developed by Nokia's research centers in Finland was seen as a potential breakthrough by its engineers that would have given the world's biggest maker of mobile phones a powerful advantage in the fast-growing smart phone market."[15]

So, it was not that Nokia had insufficient time, resources, or knowledge to pursue the next wave of products (though enormous ramping up of capabilities would have been required). The hesitancy to invest heavily enough, soon enough, allowed Apple, Research In Motion of Canada (the maker of BlackBerry phones), Samsung and LG of South Korea, and others to jump out in front in pursuit of the next profit pool.

This is a case where adherence to the design principles of the Great Repeatable Models fell one principle at a time, like dominos. It started with internal resistance to a major assault on the next-generation phone despite available technology and enthusiastic bench scientists early in the market development. It soon rippled into an eroding differentiation in the core business model and its flagship product.

Our research shows that many of the Great Repeatable Model companies that stalled out due to a disruptive innovation had ample time to react, resources to deploy, and a mortal threat to motivate them. Moreover, in most cases the disruption did not replace the entire business model or the fundamentals of customers' needs. Rather, it changed a couple of major ways that those needs could be served, while still leaving lots of elements of the repeatable model of the past that could be built on.

This is what happened in the transformation of IBM to a company centered on services and software. It is what happened in the shift of the model for Marvel Entertainment from comic books to movies using the same characters and stories.[16] The key is not usually to discard the entire model of the past, but to invest aggressively in those elements (the phone, the camera technology, the delivery vehicle for Spider-Man) that are changing. We realize that this is easier to say than to do.

The work of Christensen around the innovator's dilemma highlighted the many barriers to change that exist in a successful organization.[17] But in most cases, the truth is that there was nothing threatening the entire business model—just parts of it. We would still take a Great Repeatable Model as the starting point for growth and deal with the demons of adaptation, rather than take a model that is the pattern of no pattern and deal with strangling complexity and lack of clarity.

Delivering Enduring Advantage

As we noted earlier, there's an interesting paradox about Great Repeatable Models. On the face of it, the advantage they deliver ought not to be very durable. Their differentiation is stark. Their values and organizational structure are usually well publicized. Case after case gets written about the likes of Apple, Singapore Airlines, NIKE, Toyota, and IKEA. It still seems somewhat remarkable that Toyota has a history of allowing outside groups to study its factories and production system. This brings us back to a question that people often ask: How can companies like IKEA deliver their sustainable competitive advantage year in and year out if everyone knows their secrets?

We've identified three answers that jointly and severally explain why Great Repeatable Models stay ahead:

By compressing the distance between management and the front line. First, and this may seem paradoxical, the very simplicity of the Great Repeatable Model raises a barrier to entry. As companies move into new businesses and markets, they grow, their risks and uncertainties multiply, and the claims on managerial attention increase. At the same time, they face growing competition from new sources. All these external realities tend to create more and more organizational complexity—more systems, more measures, more conditions, more special products, more processes, more coordinators at the interfaces. As a result, the company's leadership becomes ever more distanced from the front lines of the business. This is where the features of the Great Repeatable Model prove so powerful. Great Repeatable Model leaders don't have to make so many decisions themselves if the people in the organization, like Admiral Nelson's crews, all understand the value proposition, the values, and the trade-offs—which is much more likely if they are simple and clear to begin with. Leaders can, instead, engage in the kind of external focus on customer trends and market evolution that will help them more quickly recognize important factors and threats that demand immediate response. Perhaps if Nokia's leaders had retained that external focus and had not been as absorbed, as it appears, in the need to manage internal complexities, the company might still be the undisputed leader in mobile telecommunications.

By deciding better and faster. In a world where the pace of change is increasing, the ability to decide and act more effectively than adversaries—to stay inside their decision cycle—is an enormous advantage both in the field and in targeting innovation resources faster and more precisely. It is at the heart of accelerating the delivery of results in complex markets and organizations. Great Repeatable Models are well placed to compete in this environment. Their learning processes help them recognize change early, their strongly rooted cultures enable them to reach consensus on a course of action quickly, and their trust in employees makes it possible for people on the front line to make decisions more quickly, based on better information.

By mastering the art of continuous improvement. Anyone with a background in finance knows that small differences compound to make very big ones. The famous golfer Tiger Woods had an outstanding year in 2009, winning an amazing eight of the twenty tournaments he entered. By contrast, 2010 was his worst year ever. If you look at the details of his shot-making statistics in these two dramatically different years, shown in table 1-1, you can see that his big fall-off in performance was explained by narrow differences in a few key

TABLE 1-1

Tiger Woods: small differences in repeatability, big differences in results

	2009	2010
Greens hit in regulation	68.5%	64.1%
Putts from 10 feet made	90.4%	87.3%
Driving (on fairway)	64.3%	57.2%
Three-putt greens	2.0%	2.8%
Scoring average	68.1	70.3
Tournaments won	8 (of 20)	0 (of 17)

Source: http://www.tigerwoods.com.

performance statistics. The same thing happens in business. If a company could—through a superior system for continuous feedback and improvement—reduce overhead by just 15 basis points (0.15 percent) per year better than competitors and at the same time reduce variable costs by just 30 basis points (0.3 percent) per year, over ten years this would increase its value (all else equal) relative to competition by nearly 50 percent—with about four-fifths from earning improvements and the rest from higher market value per dollar of earnings. This is why even Albert Einstein cited compound interest as the most powerful force in the universe.

The advantages that flow from a simple business model are powerful even in a stable industry. They are, however, trump cards in industries that are highly dynamic, in which other sources of competitive advantage—scale, dedicated distribution channels—can swiftly become liabilities. And these days, industries are becoming more rather than less dynamic.

Consider this regarding the speed of change: it took radio thirty-eight years to reach 50 million people; television only thirteen years; the Internet four years; and Facebook just two years. Foxconn, the Taiwan-based outsource manufacturer of the iPhone, began its business in the 1970s but really took off in 2000. Today, the company has more than $62 billion in revenues and has just exceeded the amazing level of 1 million employees—more than the combined employment at Apple, Sony, Microsoft, Dell, Intel, and HP. It continues to grow at a rate of about 100,000 new employees per year. To put this in perspective, manufacturing employment in the entire U.S. computer sector is 165,000—lower than it was even in 1975.

In this complicated world, keeping your business simple is a tremendously powerful advantage.

The Structure of This Book and Its Promise to the Reader

This book has a simple structure and an even simpler message. Hopefully, it is a metaphor for our topic of the power of simplicity in a world of escalating complexity, the silent killer of sustained and profitable growth. Most systems deal with complexity by adding more—more systems, more measures, more internal meetings, more units, more custom products, more unique processes, more new initiatives, more coordinators at the interfaces, and on and on. Our belief is that for more companies, the antidote to escalating complexity—and to the greater distance between management and the reality at the front line—is simplification, creating greater focus and liberating energy.

Chapters 2, 3, and 4 examine each of the design principles one by one and draw out the implications for people managing businesses, illustrated with many examples of practices from successful businesses with repeatable models. (Appendix 2 provides a repeatability model diagnostic that you can use to assess your degree of repeatability relative to other companies.) Chapter 5 examines what we refer to as the strategic "dilemma of the CEO" trying to balance the framework of the model with the freedom to act and change. Finally, chapter 6 concludes with a short summary of our main findings and some reflections on the epidemic of complexity that a world of constant change has inflicted on companies and how to allow simplicity to triumph.

Principle 1:
A Well-Differentiated Core

"A package must save more than it costs" is the bold statement of principle made by Ruben Rausing when he founded Tetra Pak in 1951. Tetra Pak was named after the Greek word *tetra*, meaning "four," stemming from its first core product, which was a tetrahedron-shaped package for the storage of cream. Today, Tetra Pak is one of the leading packaging companies in the world, having hit a level last year of more than 150 billion packs of all shapes and sizes and contents sold in more than 170 markets globally. It is the story of the replication of a superior business model.

The company that Rausing built is based, at its core, on three differentiating features that create competitive advantage for Tetra Pak against rival forms of packaging. First, Tetra Pak's folded laminate packages extend the shelf life of the products they contain and eliminate the costly need for refrigeration along the value chain. The second differentiation is that the shapes these folded laminate packages can take—squares and pyramids—stack more efficiently in trucks and on shelves than rounded cans or exotic bottles, thus providing another source of savings. Finally, the packaging machines that use the unique laminated material (which took nearly ten years to make commercially viable) lend themselves to high-volume dairy operations. These three features confer on Tetra Pak a competitive advantage so that the package more than compensates for the cost of buying it.

Tetra Pak is an example of a Great Repeatable Model that has grown profitably and consistently, adapting its formula and reapplying it over and over. At its core are a few unique features that determine its appeal to customers and that block competitors from emulation. Like Tetra Pak, many of the other Great Repeatable Models that we examine in this book—NIKE, IKEA, Louis Vuitton, Singapore Airlines, Enterprise Rent-A-Car, Amazon.com, and Apple—all have clear differentiations that jump right out at you. Moreover, the examples of renewal using the ideas of repeatable models also begin with a couple of areas of differentiation that formed the launchpad for rejuvenation.

Figure 2-1 contains results from our analysis of performance drivers in our two hundred–company database. As you can see, we judged that 93 percent of the top 20 percent of performers have a strong form of differentiation in their core, which creates their competitive advantage in the marketplace. This differentiation was three times as strong and clear as in the bottom 30 percent of performers.

Clarity and agreement around the uniqueness of a company, its root source of competitive advantage, and a rigorous view of its full potential to grow sound like an obvious requirement to run a business—like having a map, a mode of transport, and a destination before beginning a trip. But in our experience, this is not as common as you might think. Sometimes the press of quarterly targets and daily crises dilutes the time spent on the fundamentals. Sometimes a management team takes the

FIGURE 2-1

Adherence to design principle 1: a well-differentiated core

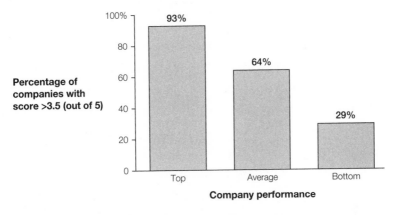

Source: Bain 200 Company Database of Repeatable Models.

strength and uniqueness of the company's value proposition for granted, usually to its peril. Sometimes, the company's differentiation is simply never on the agenda and you find that everyone has a different perspective on it. There are many reasons for cloudy self-awareness, which is why we feel that an uncommon level of clarity and simplicity around what makes a company and its business model unique is the first building block of good strategy and at the heart of the Great Repeatable Models—a clear distinctiveness that is easily understood.

One study we conducted surveyed executives and customers across a range of industries and asked how strongly differentiated the product or service was. We found that while about 80 percent of executives felt their offering was highly differentiated, only about 8 percent of their customers actually agreed with them.[1] Even as individuals, we sometimes find it quite difficult to see ourselves clearly in all of our glorious uniqueness. We hold in our stomachs near mirrors, favor our "good side," ask for compliments from those we know will give them. And that is just for our outside; imagine how much we deceive ourselves about the inside and our capabilities. This tendency is called *confirmation bias* and has been widely studied by researchers in psychology.[2]

So, it is not surprising that businesses—with hundreds of products, thousands of employees, dozens of capabilities, and a constant churn of executives who are endlessly bombarded by distractions—have difficulties in seeing their differentiation and agreeing on it or its root cause. A review that we conducted at Bain & Company looked at the nature of the key findings across 115 different strategy studies done with clients. By a wide margin, the primary insight was that the business had more potential in its core model and unique capabilities than it had recognized. It proves at the level of the organization, as endless psychologists have demonstrated for individuals, that self-awareness is often not that easy to achieve and maintain.

Effectory is the leading business in Europe in the field of employee surveys. The firm summarized for us its database of about three hundred thousand responses from many companies and from employees at all levels regarding employee awareness of differentiation and strategy. The results showed that more than half of employees do not believe that their management even "decently propagates" the stated strategy and values of the company, and that 54 percent do not believe that they understand the basics of the strategy they are supposed to be following. Some companies scored well below 20 percent, with frontline employees (those interacting with customers) having the lowest scores of all.

From Adam Smith's example of specialization in pin manufacturing increasing productivity by two hundred and fortyfold all the way to Michael Porter's treatise "What Is Strategy?", differentiation has been at the core of the definition of strategy in business.[3] Differentiation is about the unique strengths that underlie your competitive advantage. Strategy is about obtaining the full potential of these assets and capabilities by adapting and applying them to the right range of opportunities.

Differentiation is the vessel that holds the crown jewels of a business. Making money in business depends on achieving competitive superiority through these differences. It is seldom about the serial search for new, hot markets. The typical market has five to seven relevant competitors, of which two—those with the strongest and most unique models—generally capture more than 70 percent of the profit pool (returns above the cost of capital) and therefore can outinvest the others. The math of how value concentrates in a few leaders can be pushed further. From 1999 to 2009, the top-performing 10 percent of companies multiplied investor capital by an annual rate of 14 percent, while the other 90 percent achieved only a 1 percent annual rate of growth in shareholder value. This means that the best 10 percent of companies (a large percentage of which have the attributes of repeatable models) captured more than 85 percent of the market value created in the world during this period.

We will now examine the three components of our first design principle, a well-differentiated core:

- The source of differentiation and the activity system that supports it

- A well-defined method to repeat success in new situations

- A set of target markets and segments in which to reapply your model

How Businesses Differentiate

Businesses differentiate themselves from their competitors in three broad ways: superior cost economics, unique product features, or control over a key position in a larger economic system.

Low cost was the dominant differentiating feature in about 60 percent of the Great Repeatable Model companies that we studied. The companies in this group typically achieved differentiation through cost position in at least one of three ways: (1) economies of scale and the ability to achieve higher levels of productivity in manufacturing (e.g., ArcelorMittal), (2) superior supply chain management of a set of vendors (e.g., Wal-Mart, Li & Fung), and (3) pure network economics (e.g., Vodafone). Unique product and service features were the dominant form of differentiation in about 30 percent of cases. These were most often driven by brand (e.g., Virgin's set of businesses), patentable product features (e.g., Apple's iPad), or superior service levels (e.g., Singapore Airlines' first class). Control over a network, a key resource, or a command position in a larger economic system was the third and least common primary form of differentiation—only about 10 percent of companies (e.g., Microsoft's operating system). We determined the primary and secondary forms of differentiation industry by industry. Some markets—like specialty sauces, designer neckties, or publishing—consist of small niches where product differentiation is clearly at the top of the list, sometimes supplemented by a strong cost position. In other markets, we looked at margin structure and customer purchase criteria. Where margins were low and customers' first choice depended on price—an example would be low-end business hotels or airport car rentals—we recognized cost management and pricing as paramount.

But this classification of primary and secondary differentiation alone is too simplistic. To really understand how a Great Repeatable Model differentiates its business model relative to competitors', you must ask two additional sets of questions:

How do all the relevant differentiations reinforce one another? How do they work together to define a business model that can be replicated? For example, Singapore Airlines, which we discussed earlier, is legendary among business travelers for its service levels (the result of a complex and differentiated activity system encompassing everything from recruitment to in-air routines). Yet, among its main competitors, Singapore Airlines is also among the lowest-cost airlines. These two interlocking forms of differentiation propel the company's success. Its cost position without the service levels would substantially reduce loyalty and load factors. Yet, its service without the cost advantage would alter the ability to outearn and outinvest competitors.

What are the assets and capabilities at the heart of this differentiation? This second question is even more important than the first. To really understand the success of Singapore Airlines requires drilling down a level or two into the deeper sources of the differentiation, the company's robustness, and how difficult it is for competitors to emulate. Few executives to whom we have spoken during this project deny that differentiation is the cornerstone of strategy, yet the evidence shows that most management teams do not agree on the crown jewels of their company and the precise origins of their unique strengths. If that is true, imagine how difficult it is for frontline employees to understand and embrace those strengths.

Despite differentiation's central importance to strategy, we were surprised to find few systematic examinations of its sources and even of its definition. It has become one of those words that everyone uses but no one understands. As a result, we did some primary research on sources of differentiation. We used our two hundred–company database to identify more than two hundred fifty distinct forms of differentiation. We then sorted those into fifteen clusters—separate dimensions along which a business can be differentiated and that form the unique fingerprint of a company.

These fifteen forms of differentiation are arrayed in figure 2-2, the "differentiation map," along two dimensions. One dimension that we found important strategically is whether the differentiation is primarily customer facing or not (for example, IKEA's logistics skills are not customer facing, but NIKE's capabilities in design and branding around top athletes are). The second dimension is tangibility. Here we go from tangible assets, such as a unique geographic location in a shipping lane, a low-cost manufacturing technology, or a network of efficient distribution points, to less tangible differentiators, such as Enterprise's customer relationship capabilities or a management system like the one we will describe at Danaher. The fifteen basic forms of differentiation, if viewed in groups of five or fewer, generate more than five thousand sets of differentiations. Of course, below the surface of even these fifteen categories are many subdifferentiators, as we illustrate below in the case of differentiation through a unique customer relationship that can take multiple forms. If you allow just three more specific forms of differentiation for each of our major categories, the differentiation possibilities explode to well over 1 million. There is no shortage of unique ways to be unique.

Some businesses, like Tetra Pak, Amazon, Vanguard, or Olam, began with a relatively simple business model built around few real differentiators. Over time, success spawned additional forms of differentiation and a much richer and more complex model. The fate of the successful and of the disappointed can often be traced to the ability to maintain, adapt, and add differentiations. This is an acid test of sustainable strategy.

FIGURE 2-2

The fifteen types of differentiation, with examples

Management systems	**Portfolio management and finance** Berkshire Hathaway's capital allocation out-performing the index	**M&A, JVs, and partnering** Olam's selective M&A to obtain required capabilities	**Regulatory management** Pfizer's optimization of drug development for FDA approval	**BU strategy and driving priorities** Danaher's systems to drive strategic priorities to "point of impact"	**HR management and culture** Google's culture, making it the preferred place to work for top IT talent
Operating capabilities	**Supply chain and logistics** IKEA's long-term supplier relations	**Production and operations** AB InBev's tools for reducing costs in beer production plants	**Development and innovation** P&G's program Connect + Develop	**Go-to-market** NIKE's sports icons and retail management	**Customer relationships** Enterprise's closed-loop feedback, creating the most loyal car renters
Proprietary assets	**Tangible assets** Vopak's storage terminals in high-growth seaports	**Scale** (in a well-defined business) Amazon's leadership in selling books online	**Technology and IP** ASML's systems to make the smallest/fastest computer chips	**Brand** Coca-Cola's brand	**Tied customer network** Apple's iTunes and App stores

Back-office ← → Customer-facing

Source: Bain 200 Company Database of Repeatable Models.

Dissecting the greatest strengths and areas of uniqueness of a business is important to gain a deeper understanding of the true root causes of differentiation. In our experience few management teams take the time to isolate, measure, and agree on the most important sources of differentiation—where they win with core customers and why—in a precise and data-based way. Or, if they do, they do so at a quite shallow level, not really penetrating down to the root cause. If an advantage is in unit cost, well, on exactly which elements of the P&L is this true, and why, and how defensible is that advantage? Or, if an advantage exists in speed to market, what are the processes that are superior to those of competitors, and why?

To illustrate the importance of drilling down even further to really understand the simplest essence of your source of differentiation, let's take one of the fifteen types as an example: differentiation through the nature of your customer relationships. This one form of differentiation can be achieved in many different ways.

One powerful form is deep and unique technical knowledge that becomes central to your customers' own processes. For instance, Novozymes, the world leader in industrial specialty enzymes, cocreates more than 90 percent of its new products, most of which are precisely bioengineered molecules, with a customer. A second form is deep behavioral knowledge that allows you to anticipate needs and target product marketing better than competitors. An example would be the deep data on customers and sellers that American Express has due to the unique form of its charge cards. Through its precision and focus, American Express has become a company built on repeatable models. A third major form is through systems that focus in unique ways on customer loyalty and retention. The customer feedback system of Enterprise Rent-A-Car, and the way that system drives the behavior of field operations, are an example of this. These are three of the most powerful forms of differentiation through unique customer relationships. In a sense, these companies almost become part of their customers' habits, routines, and repeatability.

After you have isolated and defined as clearly as possible your sources of differentiation, the next task is to ask why you have been able to do that and how sustainable that advantage is. This requires going at least one more layer down. So, for instance, in the case of American Express, its differentiated capabilities trace back to its customer database and the unique way that it gathers transactional data.

This process of probing three levels down for the essence of your differentiation is not that easy to do—just think of the ways your favorite restaurant is different from other restaurants and what motivates you to go there more than to other places. Sometimes, the answer might be quite simple—geography, price, a particular type of food. But, in general, it is much more complicated and involves multiple aspects that interact and reinforce each other. In central Amsterdam, there are more than three hundred restaurants within a twenty-minute walk of the home of one of the authors, with a churn of about 20 percent per year. This microcosm proves to be an intense crucible of com-petition, very Darwinian in nature, yet almost always can you see well in advance who will succeed and fail. The new entrants with only the loosest sense of differentiation lose quickly. Those that last usually have a much sharper sense of differentiation and an ability to explain what it is and why it works, we have found through personal field testing.

The ability to understand the most important elements of a business model and the process of differentiation is important also in focusing innovation. Most innovation, even much dis-ruptive innovation at the highest level, affects part of a business model but leaves the rest intact. The shift from glasses to contact lenses still left the distribution network, the basic customer needs for vision correction, and the web of eye doctors relatively similar to where they were before the shift. The shift from wired to wireless telephony caused chaos for many incumbents, yet some ultimately were able to leverage their infrastructure, customer access, brand, ability to work with regulatory agencies, and so on to prevail (for instance, KPN in the Netherlands and Telstra in Australia are examples of disruptive innovation ultimately being successfully internalized by the incumbent).

Even some of the most studied examples of incumbents losing position (Kodak, Xerox, General Motors, Nokia, Motorola, and Barnes & Noble, to name a few) are not cases of wholesale replacement of an entire business model, but of specific parts of the business model turning obsolete over time while many other elements endure and remain potentially valuable and robust. The more precise your understanding of your model and what leads to success, and the simpler your differentiation is, the more precisely you can focus innovation resources on those areas where threats and change are greatest. This is why a well-defined core differentiation, and a clear and well-articulated activity system to support and replicate it, are at the center of our first design principle—without uniqueness, you can't succeed long in the market, and without sharp self-awareness of each element, you can't easily target innovation resources.

Replicating the Model to Grow

In our study, we found that repeatable business models were central to sustained success at three different levels: across businesses, across adjacencies, and within the core market itself (see figure 2-3). Some businesses, like Vanguard, IKEA, or American Express, have grown by using their repeatable models to gain share in their original core market by offering new products, targeting more and more precise customer segments, and adding services. This is the most common application of repeatable models. Some, like NIKE or Olam, have created repeatable models that they can use not only in each market, but to enter major new markets with an adapted version of their core model. NIKE has done this by entering sport after sport, and Olam has done this by entering one agricultural product after another. The third application is a repeatable model of a multicore business, like Danaher, United Technologies Corporation (UTC), or Procter & Gamble. These companies have a coherent business and management system that they apply to every business that they are in and, for Danaher especially, use to add value to their many acquisitions. In each case, these three levels of repeatable models are central to strategy, to differentiation, and to success.

To bring these situations to life a bit more, we turn to an example of each—Vanguard (single core, simple structure), Olam (single core, complex adjacency expansion), and Danaher (multicore, multi-industry).

FIGURE 2-3

Three levels of repeatable models

– Individual business driving core growth
  ‣ Examples: Vanguard, IKEA, Tetra Pak

– Businesses moving into adjacencies by modifying their model
  ‣ Examples: Olam, NIKE, Apple

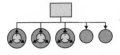

– Multicore business managing a portfolio
  ‣ Examples: Danaher, UTC, P&G

Source: Bain & Company.

The Vanguard Group: A Study in Differentiation

Figure 2-4 maps out Vanguard's primary forms of differentiation. The routines most critical to the differentiation (the shaded boxes) include its unique ownership structure, its low-cost mutual fund "engine" skewed to index funds, a distribution capability that does not rely on paying intermediaries, and a service structure that builds long-term relationships with customers. The Vanguard model is so powerful and driven so deeply into the routines that we could embellish it much further, but these are the key differentiators.

FIGURE 2-4

Vanguard's sources of differentiation

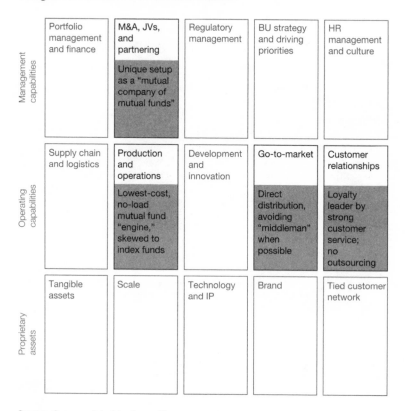

Sources: Company data; interviews with management.

Vanguard's differentiators are clear and measurable. For instance, in 1980 Vanguard's expense ratio was about half the industry average; today it is 18 percent of the average. This expense difference—perhaps another example of the mathematics of small differences and continuous improvement—accounts for a majority of the industry-leading returns of its fund portfolio. Over a ten-year period, fifty-eight of its sixty-five longest-term funds outperformed the Lipper average. Another area of strong and measurable differentiation is customer loyalty, the pillar of its strategy and internal core processes. As a measure of this, just consider that Vanguard's 2009 redemption levels (churn of customer money, a direct measure of loyalty) were only 28 percent of the industry average. These are powerful measures of differentiation.

Repeating Your Differentiation

The most successful growth strategies consist of a business model that allows the business's greatest successes to be tailored to new areas with the positive result repeated. This opportunity to replicate is one key determinant of the full growth potential of a business. Some businesses—say, the business of teaching the Dutch language—are inherently limited to locations where sufficient numbers of people want to learn this language. By contrast, a general language business with a distinct underlying architecture and technology—like the distinctive yellow boxes of Rosetta Stone—would have many more possible areas for replication by level, language, form of media, and geography.

Olam illustrates well our second level of repeatable model, predicated on a relentless movement into one new adjacent market after another (see table 2-1). The company has replicated its greatest successes in expanding into adjacent new areas of agricultural products (e.g., cashews, peanuts, almonds),

TABLE 2-1

Olam: unbroken replication for two decades

	1989	2010
Products	1 (cashew)	20
Origins	1 (Nigeria)	65
End markets	1 (Europe)	11,000 global customers
Employees	2	14,600
Financials	Nil	S$15.8B revenues
		S$450M profits
		S$6.5B equity value
		22% return on equity

Source: Company data.

new countries or regions where these products are grown (e.g., Nigeria, Indonesia, China, Australia, USA), and new value chain steps or processes to alter their character (e.g., roasting, blanching, sorting, or crushing).

CEO Sunny Verghese described the evolution of Olam's strategy:

> After our first product experience with cashews in Nigeria, we began to build operational capabilities for supply chain and risk management that we could replicate and scale across different geographies and then across different commodities. We are the only supply chain company that cross-sources multiple agricultural commodities all the way to the lowest level of aggregation at the farm gate, which increases our access, our intelligence, our speed of reaction, and provides us with a very low cost position. Perhaps the core of our business model is the risk management system for managing the risk of crop problems, pricing and currency volatility, credit and counter party risk, potential

supply disruption, and political and sovereign risk. We had to become better than anyone in the world at this, and we have. It is one of the most differentiated and most repeatable core areas of Olam. We became expert at identifying, capturing, measuring, monitoring, and addressing these risks. We could absolutely not have gone to sixty countries without this repeatable model to manage risk; it was central to our ability to scale— especially for a company that had a distributed sourcing model that reached all the way down to the level of local farms. All of the key elements of our repeatable model are in centralized functions that we can make "plug and play" for new local markets, allowing us to replicate and scale faster and better than our competitors.[4]

Olam's repeatable model (see figure 2-5, highly simplified) consists of a number of mutually reinforcing parts. These are (1) Olam's proprietary system for risk management, (2) a culture, a set of principles, and a personnel system that create a remarkable consistency (and information flow) across managers around the world that allows it to act as "one company," (3) sourcing practices "at the farm gate" to do businesses with local farmers and agents in local villages (something no one else does at this level), (4) the control of the subsequent value chain up to the "factory gate" of the world's biggest fast moving consumer goods (FMCG) companies, (5) providing value-added solutions and services to customers (e.g., traceability guarantees, organic certification, customized grades, etc.), (6) selective integration in the value chain into upstream plantations and midstream processing layered around the supply chain core based on proprietary insights as to where the global supply chain arbitrages are, and (7) the capacity to acquire and integrate small acquisitions at the local level—also quite a rare repeatable skill in the countries where Olam operates.

FIGURE 2-5

Olam's sources of differentiation

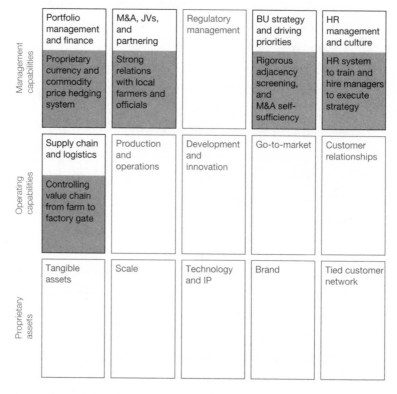

Sources: Company data; interviews with management.

As CEO Verghese recounts:

> In our first seventeen years, we did not have the skills, knowledge, capital, or confidence to do M&A. Plus we were busy growing rapidly, organically. Now we have a repeatable M&A playbook. We have done twenty-seven acquisitions in the last three years, and only one was sourced from an investment bank. Our line managers find and source these targets given the visibility that they have by leveraging our network and presence in sixtyfive countries. This is sort of a hidden asset that we had because of the fact that our people had a direct

line of sight on these targets given their understanding of our strategy. Our cross-border acquisition ability is now part of our core skills, and we manage it centrally with lots of clear rules and criteria. To do the twenty-seven acquisitions, we had a target list that we had carefully assembled of about ninety.[5]

We did a similar examination to that of Olam across our case examples to identify the primary dimensions of repetition (displayed in figure 2-6). This provides a simple starting list for management teams to use in stepping back and reflecting on where their core business model might be replicated profitably. The most common expansion paths are geographic locations (e.g., Wal-Mart's store expansion or Huawei's country expansion in telecom equipment), vertical market applications (e.g., Hilti's product expansion in drilling and fastening systems), customer segments (e.g., American Express's constant resegmenting of its market, now with more than 120 tracked segments), brand (e.g., Virgin's use of brand extension for businesses ranging from airlines to music), and technology platforms (e.g., the extension of Apple's devices, all linked to the iTunes platform).

FIGURE 2-6

Vectors of repeatability: four categories with examples

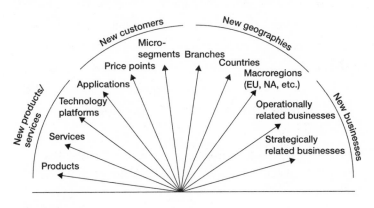

Source: Bain analysis.

In general, most growth strategies advance in several directions at once. In previous work, we looked closely at the odds of success (only 20–25 percent, on average) of the six types of growth moves that business make (new channels, new customer segments, new businesses built around a deep capability, new geographies, new products or services, and new upstream or downstream parts of the value chain).[6] These are the "subassemblies" that make up most growth plans of most businesses. We find that the moves based on new products and services to core customers have the highest probability of success. Figure 2-6 focuses on four of these six types of growth moves that we find to be the most repeatable.

Companies whose differentiations are primarily customer facing tend to grow organically and selectively. It is difficult to expand rapidly by acquisition if the essential uniqueness that you bring is based on a unique model exquisitely tailored to your core customers. A good comparison is the story of Dell versus Gateway.

In 1994, Dell was virtually the same size and stature as Gateway. Dell had $3.5 billion in revenues; Gateway had $2.7 billion. Both had identical 7 percent pretax profit margins. The market value of Dell was $2 billion, Gateway $1.7 billion. Both were using the direct model to sell personal computers in the United States, essentially constituting their entire business at that time. Yet, Dell chose an organic expansion path focused on six major countries, six major product extensions, and about the same number of unique customer segments. Expansion occurred methodically, step by step, always one step at a time from the core. Before entry, the company took great pains to design and test the variations in the base case model that would be necessary (say, moving the model from personal computers to workstations or from the United States to the United Kingdom).

By contrast, Gateway was less systematic and not at all repeatable. It entered some countries by acquisition, others organically. In some countries it built retail stores (not the direct model concept), and in others it did not. In some markets, like New Zealand, it purchased distributors to enter the market (also not a direct model). It went after as many countries as it could handle, allowing complexity to explode and engulf its economics. By the end of the decade, Dell had been voted company of the decade, and Gateway was in severe financial distress. Those close to the story see many subplots that help explain this dramatic separation of fortunes, but our view is much simpler. Gateway put growth ahead of its model—trying to adapt or capture opportunities that did not really fit—whereas Dell chose to limit its growth to opportunities that were most in accord with its distinctive model.

The economic value of a business built around a repeatable model is strongly related to how often it can be replicated successfully. The current potential of the Olam model is in proportion to the number of countries (maybe seventy to eighty), commodities (perhaps twenty to forty), and process steps (perhaps three to seven for different commodities) where the model might be immediately extended—a growth potential that we calculate to be several times the current size of the company.

When the Differentiation Is Not Only About the Customer

Most of the Great Repeatable Models that we examined in this study were built primarily on customer-facing sources of differentiation supported, obviously, by backroom processes and routines. But this is not true of all of them. Take, for example, the case of multicore businesses, which apply their repeatable model to very different types of businesses with completely different core customers. There are not many of these success stories, but the ones that have persisted are robust and profound in their lessons for other companies.

For instance, the best-performing multicore company in the world over the past twenty years, Danaher Corporation, also has one of the most well-developed repeatable management models. Despite the ravages wrought by the recession in 2009 on industrial companies, Danaher maintained its operating cash flow at $1.8 billion, 16 percent of revenues, and utilized that cash flow to do eighteen acquisitions during the year often with little competition. As a result, Danaher's stock price increased more than 30 percent during 2009. From the start of the financial crisis in mid-2008 to May 2010, the S&P 500 index declined by 18 percent; Danaher's stock improved by 10 percent. The 2009 annual report's shareholder letter gives credit for this to the Danaher Business System (DBS), a continuously evolving codification of the company's core practices and routines.

Danaher, which celebrated its twenty-fifth anniversary as a company in 2009, was founded by two brothers, Steven and Mitchell Rales, who began purchasing industrial businesses that had a strong position in a focused niche and that they felt were not achieving their full operating potential. As CEO Larry Culp says today, the brothers "wanted to make a contra-bet on U.S. manufacturing. This initial act in its own right created some of what stays with us, which is not taking things too often at face value." DBS has been more than twenty years in its evolution, starting in 1988 when the company revenues were just $715 million with 6 percent after-tax margins (versus $11.2 billion and 11 percent net margins in 2009). Danaher credits DBS both for its ability to grow the company fifteenfold over this period and especially for the ability to nearly double its margins.

The evolution of DBS began with the development of a lean manufacturing management system at one of its first

portfolio companies—Jacobs Vehicle Systems (a brake manufacturer famous for the Jake Brake, still the leader in compres-
sion braking systems for diesel engines). Danaher management
recognized that it had developed its own version of the Toyota
Production System and began to apply it successfully to its
other businesses, and to use it as a catalyst to drive value in new
acquisitions. Since then (see figure 2-7) the system has evolved
to include an increasing number of business activities where the
principles of efficient process flow can improve performance.
While initially focused almost exclusively on cost and productivity, the system has evolved recently to include processes also
focused on accelerating organic growth.

Figure 2-8 illustrates our analysis of the Danaher repeatable
model and its differentiations at the level of the entire corporation, which include a superior method to target and make acquisitions, an integration program for the acquisitions using DBS that
has a proven record for margin improvement within two years, the

FIGURE 2-7

Development of the Danaher Business System (DBS)

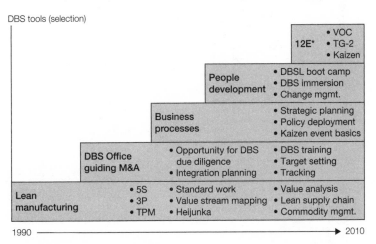

*12E=Idea to execute
Note: Timing is illustrative (i.e., not exact).
Source: Company materials.

FIGURE 2-8

Danaher's sources of differentiation and supporting activities

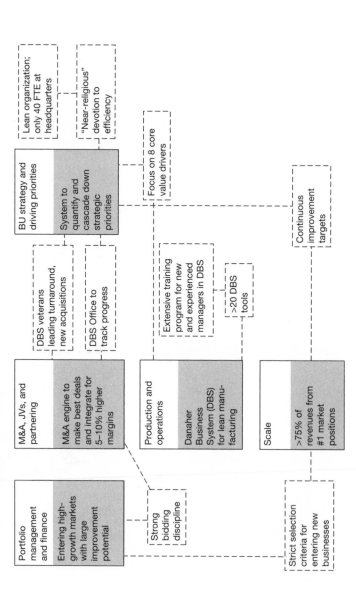

Source: Company data; interviews with management.

use of DBS to manage the businesses in a rigorous and consistent manner, and a set of tools for continuous productivity improvement in R&D, go-to-market activities, the plant, supply chain, and backroom operations. Each of these is quite specific and measurable in its effect. Here, we have embellished the differentiation map one step further, adding enabling activities that contribute to the differentiation and are at the heart of DBS. We recommend using this form of the chart as a tool for a management team to define and agree on where and how and why it is differentiated, how the pieces fit together, and where there are convincing measures that the sources of unique advantage are still robust.

Our discussions with CEO Larry Culp about how DBS works in practice reveal a surprising insight. First, the system is so integrated into the company that it is almost self-propelling, with operating managers able to share results and learning horizontally across the company. DBS is the mainspring of the experience curve that is clearly at work in this company—whose unit of experience might be seen as years of management with DBS times the number of businesses where it is applied. Second, the corporate headquarters for this company of 48,000 people and more than 80 businesses contains fewer than 50 people—about half of them in charge of codifying and propelling DBS. This group, called the Danaher Business System Office, is modeled after the Toyota Production System Office, reports directly to the CEO, and is charged with doing internal diagnostics of potential, codifying success stories and new tools, and lubricating the natural learning process.

Acquisitions account for a majority of Danaher's growth and are a key area of application of repeatable models and of the Danaher Business System. Culp's explanation of what happens with a new acquisition at Danaher shows the ubiquitous role of DBS:

> When you boil it down, simplicity, focus, and repeatability are at the heart of everything. You can see this in the three things that we do with a newly acquired

business. First, we expose them to as many of our tools of DBS as we possibly can in a very practical way—not in a classroom. We take the leadership team for weeks to see our factories, go into our labs, sit in on management team meetings, and to sense and smell the rigor and repeatable discipline in ways that cannot be described in a document. We then have them do hands-on *kaizen* work—sometimes in the factory or sometimes in another part of the business—in order to begin to absorb the tools, culture, and unifying vocabulary fully.[7]

Second, we insist that within the first one hundred days we have a shared strategic plan for the business following the very specific blueprint of DBS. Our system tries to keep it simple, often simpler than it ever was before—What game are we playing? What is the context? How can we win against key competitors? How high is high? Where do we start? In general, we find that our process increases focus on the core in about 60 percent of the time versus what it was when we bought the company. We like going a mile deep and less broad. We emphasize the economics of niches and how attractive 4× relative share in a focused area could really be.[8] Finally there is the human element, where, through this process, we shape the team that can implement the plan.[9]

Danaher's data shows a consistent ability to improve the margins of acquisitions, often by as much as 5–10 percent of revenues, by applying DBS. It is the key reason why analysts give it a *conglomerate premium* (valuation higher than the sum of the parts). Culp summarized: "Without DBS, we would struggle to achieve economies of scale."[10]

Practice Makes Perfect

A Bain & Company study of 742 companies across 18,653 acquisitions during the period 1987–2006 found a strong correlation between deal pattern and returns. Three major patterns were studied: frequent acquirers (especially those doing multiple acquisitions per year), infrequent acquirers (those doing no more than a deal every two years), and binge acquirers (those doing many acquisitions in a very short period, such as during the Internet bubble).

The result showed that frequent acquirers had "excess" returns (relative to their cost of capital) that were 2–3 points per year higher than the infrequent acquirers' and 3–4 points higher than the binge acquirers'. Frequent acquirers that ramped up their frequency over the period (presumably gaining ability through learning and repeatability) did the best of all, with nearly 2 points of annual return better than that of the average frequent acquirer. These differences might sound modest. However, over a ten- to twenty-year period, a difference of 2–4 points in shareholder return per year accumulates powerfully.[11]

During the period of the study, General Electric led the list of the successful and frequent acquirers, with 564 acquisitions, 28 per year (the largest share for the creation of GE Capital). GE, of course, has one of the best repeatable methods for doing small to medium "tuck in" acquisitions. Examples of other frequent acquirers showing the ramp-up pattern and very high excess returns include Cemex (Mexican cement consolidator), Johnson & Johnson (J&J), Danaher, and Medtronic.[12]

Danaher's approach is mirrored by United Technologies Corporation (UTC), which has a system called Achieving Competitive Excellence (ACE) that it applies to all businesses and uses to guide adding value to acquisitions. ACE had its origins in 1989 with a project to understand why the Otis Elevonic 401 elevators had quality problems requiring in-service callbacks of up to forty per year—eighty times higher than benchmarks. The answer led UTC to a series of shop floor practices drawn from the best Japanese manufacturers at the time. ACE also evolved toward applications beyond the shop floor and into backroom operations, as well as customer management. ACE results are made quite public. In a recent annual review, UTC cited 908 ACE sites across the world, as well as the percentage rated at levels from gold to silver to bronze and below.

Two factors in our study of conglomerates explained their performance differences the most. One was the percentage of revenues in businesses with leadership economics (Danaher, ITT, P&G, J&J, and UTC have about 60–70 percent of revenues from leadership or coleadership positions). The other was the presence of a deep and well-developed corporate-level repeatable model—usually a model to make acquisitions, improve, and manage them—that formed the core of the strategy.

A case in point is the growth of AB InBev. In its 1999 annual report, AB InBev (then called Interbrew) touted the thirty acquisitions it had made during the prior decade and its growth to a level of $4 billion, with operating margins (EBITDA) of 23 percent. Today, the company has grown to $36 billion, with an astonishing margin of 38 percent. The growth remains heavily through acquisition—especially of the South American leader AmBev in 2004 and then the U.S. leader Anheuser-Busch in 2008.

AmBev in itself is a remarkable story of a private equity firm's purchase during the 1980s of an underperforming beer company built around its brand Brahma. The group developed some unique approaches to operational excellence embodied it in three well-defined repeatable systems (that we discuss again in chapter 3 when we talk about the power of routines). AmBev ultimately captured almost three-fourths of the Brazilian beer market and began to introduce with success its formula throughout South America. For instance, one element of its formula is called Voyager Plant Optimization (VPO). Each brewery is (or is not) certified as VPO compliant, given a score, and tracked in detail on a transparent and comparable set of metrics across all breweries worldwide. This is not a huge corporate program, but, as with Danaher, is described by AB InBev as "owned directly by the plants." Thanks to differentiations like the VPO, AB InBev was well on target for the annual $2.25 billion cost savings it had projected for its 2008 purchase of U.S. brewing giant Anheuser-Busch.

Conglomerates in the developing economies are partial exceptions. There you often find that a larger percentage of the best-performing companies are multicore companies, such as Reliance, Tata, Larsen & Toubro, and the Aditya Birla Group in India. In these instances, we found additional and more fundamental sources of differentiation at work to propel the company's success, such as the ability to deal with complex and sometimes inscrutable government departments, to obtain financing at a reasonable rate (not easy in the volatile earlier stages of development), and to hire and manage large numbers of people in a disorganized labor market. Such fundamental capabilities were often cited by executives in these companies as key strengths and differentiations explaining their relative success rates. As companies and economies mature, we find that the most differentiating routines begin to move down from these big, relatively high-level capabilities to resemble developed world conglomerates like Danaher or UTC.

When companies do get into trouble because they move too far away from their core differentiation or grow in a manner inappropriate to it, the answer often lies in returning to the original formula. Indeed, our book *Profit from the Core* is based on studying hundreds of companies that prematurely abandoned their core, failed to see its full potential, and lived to regret their mistake.[13] Let's look at an example.

Back to the Bricks: How LEGO Group Rediscovered Its Magic

If you were looking for a visual image for repeatability, you would be hard pressed to find one better than a set of LEGO bricks or systems, embodying the universal appeal that earned LEGO the mantle of toy of the century for the 1900s. Yet, the repeatability of the physical product was in stark contrast to the strategy the company began to follow in the 1980s and '90s. CEO Jørgen Vig Knudstorp explained:

> The founder of LEGO, Ole Kirk Kristiansen, was a carpenter who made houses and furniture, including miniatures of his furniture. When the Depression happened in 1932, he could not sell as much furniture as he needed, so he started making wooden toys to boost his income. He was a colorful character in his neighborhood and had a reputation for always making fun in the workplace, hence the name LEGO, which comes from two Danish words, *leg godt*, meaning "play good." Over the years he developed, and his son later perfected, the unique precision interlock of the plastic molded bricks, which, to this day, remains a competitive advantage. The result of their work was an "automatic binding brick" with the "holy of holies" in the business, clutch

power. After more than seven years in the making, they filed for a patent in 1958 for the basic eight-studded LEGO Brick that has not changed since then. When the wooden factory burned in 1960, the son decided to focus on only making plastic bricks. Every one of the seven thousand pieces binds as [if] glued, and [they] do not fall apart. That is the essence of the scalability of the product and the platforms on which brick sets are created.

He wanted to be the best, not the biggest, and to stay with his core philosophy and his core brick product, which he did until his death. In the mid-1970s his grandson, Kjeld Kirk Kristiansen, took over and extended further the strategy of the repeatable model, driving revenues from $100 million in 1978 to $1.3 billion by 1993. In 1994 he had to step down due to personal health. Subsequent waves of managers took a different course, driving a strategy of moving into more than five adjacencies every year, shifting from toys to a "brand company." LEGO Group entered theme parks, clothing, television programming, watches, publications, and learning labs. As a result, the company entered a ten-year period of declining performance that saw the profit margin go from 15 percent in 1993 to negative 28 percent in 2004. Over this period, LEGO Group lost value at an average rate of three hundred thousand euros per day. This was the situation that confronted me when I took over as CEO in 2004.[14]

Knudstorp and his team embarked on a three-phased, seven-year plan: stabilize the company and generate cash, build a defensible set of core products, and position for new growth. They did this by returning to the core differentiation, shedding most of the distracting adjacencies, and betting on their ability to renew and adapt the original LEGO model. Here's Knudstorp again:

> My concern as new CEO was that the model was becoming obsolete. We faced a low-cost producer. We wondered if we were world class in manufacturing anymore and whether our differentiation really mattered. How strong, really, was our customer franchise? What we discovered was enormous potential in rejuvenating the core model, where the major components of that renovation have been new systems to refocus on the customer, initiatives around technologies of digitalization and microchips we could build into the blocks, and globalization. We needed a new repeatable business model to evolve. As a company, we had led the revolution from wood to plastic, did not fully take advantage of the potential of the microchip for our product, but now digitalization provides the next wave of adaptation for us. You can build houses online and then order the exact set from LEGO Design by Me, or you can start with the physical product and move it digitally. We have even put into our business development the mandate— if it is not a repeatable model, then don't even bother.[15]

LEGO Group is a powerful example of a business that rediscovered the unrecognized potential in its historic differentiation. It also shows how to renew and adapt a winning formula that had gotten lost through strategic errors. Sure enough, LEGO's core business has snapped back in place. In 2009, net profits increased 63 percent and pretax profit margin rose to 24 percent—a far cry from the enormous losses of the previous decade. At the same time, revenues grew at 25 percent, compared with flat industry sales, driving up global market share for LEGO. Beyond the financials is a more customer-oriented culture, a shortened distance between the CEO and the front line, a 50 percent more rapid product development time, and an outpouring of new, innovative products like a virtual LEGO world and a Disney licensing agreement to create Toy Story LEGO sets.

Failure to see the full potential of your core and its differentiation is not uncommon. It can have three major effects, none of them good. First, it reduces your ability to see opportunities near your core. Second, it clouds your ability to know where to invest to keep the core differentiation alive. Finally, it may even give you false confidence to enter businesses for which your skills are unsuited. Such reasons are probably behind the entropy and enormous stock price decline of Starbucks before the founder returned to again set it right. They underlie Procter & Gamble's stall-out and movement into unsuccessful adjacencies like pharmaceuticals and cosmetics before A. G. Lafley took over as CEO in 2000, righted the ship, and rejuvenated its repeatable model. These factors also underlie most of the disappointing adjacency moves cataloged in our book *Beyond the Core*.[16]

Though LEGO is a particularly vivid example of temporary loss of self-awareness, it is not at all unique.

Some Ideas to Get You Started

Though all strategy starts with differentiation, with the crown jewels that create competitive advantage for a company, in our experience most businesses do not have a very good handle on their real, measurable source of differentiation; have not put the pieces together explicitly; have not collected the data in a rigorous manner; and do not talk about it that much in management meetings. It is a bit like the couple who have not discussed their relationship in years, only to one day realize the old assumptions they once held no longer hold. Not a good formula for lasting success.

Here are three simple ideas to begin to get a better handle on where you are really differentiated. First, ask each of your top fifteen managers privately what they consider the most differentiated and important assets and capabilities, and how they could prove this in a measurable way against a competitor. You might be surprised at the variety of responses. Second, look at the past twenty growth investments you have made, do an honest rating of their success levels, and then try to determine what the successes and the disappointments each have in common. This is often a startling piece of analysis and a real clue to differentiation. Finally, diagram the "activity system" of your most important business and ask where the differentiation is stable, where it is weak and needs to be strengthened, and where capabilities need to be added. Compare that with the top five initiatives in your current plan. If a gap exists, you know where to start.

For a multicore business, it is certainly worthwhile considering these ideas for all of your most important businesses. However, we would add one further idea, which is to ask, what is the repeatable model by which the "center" adds value? Is it as convincing and as clearly structured as some of the ones we discuss in this book, like Danaher's, AB InBev's, and Procter & Gamble's? Should it be?

One final thought—occasionally open this book to this spot, even just once a year, and ask yourself the following questions about your own business or the business you are most concerned about. Then reflect on the quality and rigor of your answer in light of our discussion of differentiation:

- What are your primary sources of differentiation? Are they gaining in strength or waning in strength? How do you *really* know?

- Does the full management team agree on them? Would frontline employees have the same list? If not, why?

- What is the success rate from extending your repeatable model to new markets and situations? Are you happy with that? What explains the successes and failures?

- What will be the key differentiators of the future? Are you building world-class capabilities in areas where you perceive gaps?

- What is the full potential of the differentiation and the repeatable model that exploits it? Where can it be best extended? How do you decide?

Now, onward, to the discussion of the second of our three design principles of the Great Repeatable Models: the ability to identify a manageable number of deep principles and beliefs at the center of the company and its strategy, and to drive them into "nonnegotiables" and specific routines to implement through the organization.

Principle 2: Clear Nonnegotiables

Have you ever watched a school of herring in the ocean change direction in the blink of an eye, as if the entire group were a single organism rather than thousands of individual fish? For instance, herring under attack from puffins shift instantly into elaborate layered schooling of different shapes for predator evasion with names like hourglass, vacuole, and split. Imagine if your front-line organization could react this rapidly and precisely.

Scientists have been studying self-organizing populations—from ants to flocks of birds—that act in concert without missing a beat to debate or coordinate. The result is *swarm theory*—the study of how large populations act in unison to accomplish tasks like finding food, escaping danger, or colonizing new homes. Swarm theory has shown how incredibly coordinated behaviors involving thousands of separate agents can often be reduced to a small number of feedback cues and simple decision rules that all follow.

One scientific survey notes, "One key to an ant colony, for example, is that no one's in charge. No generals command ant warriors. No managers boss ant workers. The queen plays no role except to lay eggs. Even with half a million ants, a colony functions just fine with no management at all—at least none that we would recognize. It relies instead upon countless interactions between individual ants, each of which is following simple rules of thumb. Scientists describe such systems as self-organizing."[1] For instance, when a group from one species of ant encounters an enemy, group members give off a strong but short-lasting pheromone into the air that other, more distant ants sense. The ants receiving this chemical signal immediately pursue it until the enemy is disabled, stopping the emission and the stream of reinforcements. Through such simple routines, ants have become the ultimate survivors and adaptors—indeed, the biomass of ants in the world may be greater than that of human beings.[2]

Some businesses have borrowed from these discoveries. For instance, American Air Liquide coordinates the routes of its large truck fleet delivering gas using swarm theory–based models. Southwest Airlines has tested "ant-based models" to coordinate landings at some of its small airports. Although some firms have used simple, swarm theory–like rules for operational problems, it is mostly the Great Repeatable Model firms that seem to be able to apply, often unconsciously like nature's swarms, a set of principles to the whole organization in a way that results in self-organizing behavior. It is this application of swarm theory to strategy—through the ubiquity of a few simple rules driving complex, but coordinated behavior—that constitutes the second design principle of the Great Repeatable Model.

To understand the power of this principle, you have to understand that from the moment a business is founded, there begins a process by which the CEO becomes ever more distant from the customer and from the front line. Messages and information up and down the organization slow down and grow increasingly distorted. It is the corporate equivalent of the classic "telephone game," where each person around a table whispers the same message to the person on his or her left, only to find the message unrecognizable when it finds its way back around. When companies respect the second principle, this distortion is less likely to happen. The reason is threefold. First, a common point of view, core beliefs, and vocabulary improve the ability to communicate. Second, the self-organization that can occur through shared principles permits a simpler organization with fewer layers, fewer handoffs, and shorter communication lines, all of which reduce the distortion of messages. Finally, information in the other direction—from the front line and the customer—is less likely to become trapped or distorted for these same reasons. The result should be an organization in which all the employees are more in tune, with a shorter distance from the CEO to the front line.

Let's start now by looking at what the translation of a strategy and its key initiatives into "nonnegotiables" might look like.

Consider this discussion with the new CEO of a large, iconic European company after a factory visit during his first one hundred days on the job:

> The manager was presenting a restructuring plan, where we were consolidating some manufacturing lines. He was to transfer some of his production to our factory in Germany. In his plan, he showed that there would be a six-month deterioration of customer service, but then things would improve again back to current service levels. I said that I was shocked that he was presenting a plan that actually forecasts lower levels of service. I asked him why he could possibly believe this was acceptable. He replied, "It is simple math really. Your office has only

given me two instructions: move factory production offshore and make it cash neutral—i.e., no inventory builds. The only way I can do that is to cut customer service. You do the math." It made me realize that unless I could put in place some basic nonnegotiables of how we do business, we would be taking actions against our customers all the time. And often under my name!

My view of nonnegotiables is simple—it is a contract between me and the front line. If we force them to be traded off to achieve financial objectives, they should raise it with me directly. Now one of our nonnegotiables is, "We will only plan for increases in customer service level—never static and never decreasing." If that factory manager had this, he would have called me and said, "Do you know your own finance department has issued two separate instructions to me that will force me to decrease customer service levels? What do I do?" In most cases I would say, "Over my dead body," but I'm sure there will be a quarter where this is a tough call. But it should be my tough call. I shouldn't make our front line have to take a trade-off against our customer interests. So often, nonnegotiables are used by me to ensure that the organization is aligned on the really important issues and trade-offs—it highlights the few big issues from the millions of financial pressures we put on the business every day.

The Evidence

Perhaps the most important result from our two hundred–company study was the discovery that *the use of well-defined, shared core principles and beliefs linking to frontline behavior* was one of the parameters in our study with the highest correlation to business performance, along with a few other factors such as focus around a well-defined core. This is a key finding of our research and a central motivating purpose for this book. We believe that this should affect how companies craft strategy for changing markets.

Figure 3-1 shows that well-recognized, behavior-driving, shared principles and beliefs throughout the *whole* organization were rated at 4–5 (on a 1 to 5 scale) for 83 percent of our best-performing quintile of businesses, versus only 26 percent for the worst performers. Combine that with the fact that three of every four of the top performers had a repeatable model, versus only one in eight for the worst performers, and you see the power of our second design principle in explaining performance.

More self-organizing behavior, if done consistently, can increase the speed of a business. If you do things faster, you can capture more new growth opportunities ahead of competitors and accomplish more per unit of time, hence faster growth. If you speed up the rate of cell reproduction in a plant, it grows faster. Same for a business. It is the simple math of growth.

FIGURE 3-1

Adherence to design principle 2: clear nonnegotiables

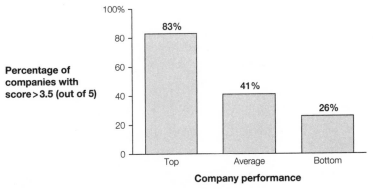

Source: Bain 200 Company Database of Repeatable Models.

Principles that create self-organizing behavior are all around us (yet, we believe, underexploited in businesses). Just think of the complex pattern of road travel in a typical city with literally millions of people behind the wheel of a powerful, lethal machine, all fighting to get where they need to go rapidly. Yet, a relatively small number of principles and nonnegotiables keeps it organized, such as road lines, the side of the road to drive on, speed limits, standard colors for lights, rules of the road, and the introduction of driver's license testing. This system is mostly self-governing, and surprisingly effective. Without well-understood principles, you would get chaos. Though the power of principles sounds like a "soft concept" connoting anodyne statements in annual reports, that is not what we mean. When used appropriately, nonnegotiables (and the routines that drive them deeper into behaviors) show why the Great Repeatable Model companies can translate strategies into action better than their more complex competitors.

As you will see, many successful businesses have developed their own approach to the power of principles. Some approaches are more general than others. Some blend core values of the founders with more behavioral nonnegotiables. Some have separate lists for strategic imperatives, for core values, and for the company's unique point of view on the laws of motion of the industry. Each should tailor this to the organization in light of its history and what its culture will embrace. These systems of clear strategic guidelines and core principles create the self-organizing behavior that is a hallmark of many of the Great Repeatable Model companies. We could offer dozens of examples, but will try to illustrate with just a few.

Introducing the Nonnegotiable

Nonnegotiables is a short phrase to describe a rich idea. The idea is to translate the most important tenets of strategy into a few prescriptive statements that people throughout the organization can understand, relate to, and use to shape actions and decisions. This "middle ground" is often where the translation of strategy into action breaks down in complex companies. We find that it is much easier to do for a business whose strategy is built around a clear, repeatable form of differentiation, as described in chapter 2. We define *nonnegotiables*, therefore, as a prescriptive statement of principle that can be used to guide managerial decisions and provide a reference point for making trade-offs. They are an effective way to translate a strategy (made up of an aspiration, a set of choices on where to play and how to win, and an activity system defining how the business is differentiated and will add value) into simple, useful, motivating instructions for the organization. They are the headlines of the "user's manual" to implementing the strategy.

We have all had user's manuals for products like cameras that seem to dive right into complex engineering detail about how each function works, without an overview in clear written language about how the machine works, the best strategy for using it, and what its full potential is. One of us has read the instruction manual for his complicated camera five times without internalizing it, and is turning now to privately written instruction books to see whether they are better than the manufacturer at describing how to get the most out of the product. Many strategies are articulated without this middle level, making them much harder to implement consistently, as with our camera manual. These intermediate "instructions" between high-level strategy and the front line are what we refer to as the nonnegotiables of strategy.

To illustrate how companies use nonnegotiables, let's consider a few examples. In chapter 2 we described the unique business model that Olam has used to repeat its successes in new countries, new commodities, and new steps of the value chain. One of Olam's key strategic pillars is its supply chains, which extend directly to the farmer in the field in the producing countries, versus its competitors who pick up the commodities on a delivered-in-store basis at the port city or customs point, relying up to there on undisciplined local systems, often rife with inefficiencies and places where money leaks out along the way. As a result, Olam today interacts with more than two hundred thousand separate suppliers across varying producing countries in the developing world. This makes Olam one of the lowest cost suppliers, as it squeezes out inefficiencies, and is better able to manage the various risks through primary data that others do not have.

Olam uses the power of principles and nonnegotiables to structure and maintain consistency across its business model. For instance, the company has developed some nonnegotiables to implement the strategic tenet that its supply chains go up to the farm gate. One is that managers must live in a rural area in a developing country to learn about what really goes on at the front line. Even the most city-bound MBA hire from a top business school must experience living in these rural areas. This nonnegotiable is supported by a set of routines, such as how these assignments are set up, criteria for hiring, and training. This practice is central to the Olam culture and is a shared bonding experience of all managers. Another nonnegotiable is the requirement that each local manager place relationships with the local farmers at the highest priority. This has led to a range of routines, some captured in the company's "field operating manual," for doing this. Olam even has created models of efficient farms through their farmer field schools which demonstrate best farm practices that can help to improve farmers' operations. In the Ivory Coast, this program improved the crop yields of local cotton farmers by more than 25 percent. Olam has been systematically building its business model around a few differentiators and clear principles that drive the strategy from its headquarters in Singapore in a consistent manner out to the farm gate in a wide range of rural communities since its start-up around a single country (Nigeria), a single commodity (cashews), and a single value chain step (collect and ship).

Toyota—older, more industrial, and more regimented than Olam by the nature of its industry—shows how strategy in a Great Repeatable Model company can be translated into a few rules and behaviors of the organization all the way out to the front line. The Toyota system has, in some sense, pioneered many of the techniques of nonnegotiables. Since its founding, Toyota has wielded its management system as a competitive weapon in the global passenger car market. At its core are the *kaizen* principles of continuous improvement and its belief that targeting zero defects also reduces cost. The Toyota system has fourteen management principles that connect behaviors and decisions throughout the organization and ultimately link to detailed processes and routines at the front line.

Take principle 5 as codified by Jeffrey Liker in *The Toyota Way*—"Build a culture of stopping to fix problems in order to get quality right the first time."[3] This nonnegotiable cascades down into practices like *andon*, where a line operator in an assembly plant, for instance, has the obligation to turn on a light above his station when he sees a problem or defect. The team leader then has less than thirty seconds (with vehicles rolling past that are being assembled at the average rate of one per minute) to decide whether to stop the line or whether the problem can be solved without doing that. To make this decision, the team leader has been trained on detailed procedures about what to do. This practice repeats across all Toyota plants, which also repeat a consistent layout and flow. Such consistency allowed Toyota for decades to harness the power of continuous improvement as a competitive advantage against rivals such as

General Motors, which historically has not had a well-developed repeatable model.

These two examples of nonnegotiables linked to the unique strategy of a business are focused mostly on operations—manufacturing and supply chain. However, some of the most important nonnegotiables can relate directly to the customer.

For instance, consider the ongoing renewal of Unilever under new CEO Paul Polman. Unilever has a strategic ambition that includes doubling in size while reducing its total environmental impact. This ambition links to a number of strategic imperatives across the company's consumer products businesses. These pillars of the strategy are set out in a construct that Unilever calls the *compass*. One part of the compass identifies the imperative of "winning in key brands through innovation." This then leads to a specific nonnegotiable (remember, this is a corporate-level strategy applying to multiple businesses) that all major investments in innovation must be focused on the most important preference drivers of target consumers determined through a method of blind testing. This, in turn, has led to the requirement to be very clear about the routines of blind testing, defining target consumers, and identifying drivers of preferences. These were worked out in "cocreation" procedures across the organization to arrive at some consistent approaches, to then communicate them, and ultimately to adjust the reward system accordingly. Results thus far have shown improvements in new launches and market performance of core brands.

Franchise businesses are forced, by the decentralized and less directly controllable nature of franchising, to specify quite clear sets of nonnegotiables that each franchisee must follow. Doing this well is at the heart of the ability to grow successfully and not lose control of processes or consistency. For instance, Belron, a company that traces its origins in the glass business back to 1897 in Cape Town, South Africa, is now the world leader in the business of vehicle glass replacement and repair. The company allows the use of local brands in each country where it operates—this is primarily a local business, and insurance practices and rules for payment vary enormously. However, the essence of the franchise agreement includes a range of well-defined nonnegotiables that the company refers to as the "Belron way of doing things." This includes especially a specific set of principles and practices for customer service, which Belron sees as a key differentiator, and which have been assembled into what Belron calls its Customer Delight Acceleration program, which consists of four tightly prescribed modules, its nonnegotiables. The program itself contains levels of detailed routines to drive this into action. One requires that every customer interaction be followed up to obtain a Net Promoter® score (NPS®) rating. These ratings are posted at the branch and are also calculated for the individual installer who arrives in your driveway to replace your windshield.

A typical problem area in this business is for people who experienced service problems. A few years ago, the NPS for these customers was 19 percent, while today, after adoption of these principles as nonnegotiables, it has risen to 67 percent. In the past five years, despite its low-growth industry, Belron has doubled in size, and even during the past two years, Belron has grown at 14 percent per year. Central to many of the most successful franchise businesses, such as Belron, McDonald's, Chick-fil-A, and RE/MAX, are a business model of striking simplicity in frontline execution and a set of nonnegotiables and routines that franchisees must follow to keep their franchise.

These four examples show how some companies with Great Repeatable Model–level performance have created and used nonnegotiables. Each has taken a core element of its strategy and business model, defined it as a set of nonnegotiable principles, and selectively driven these nonnegotiables down into frontline routines. It is in this middle area of strategy—between the concept of where to play and how to win, and the internal consistency of actually doing it—that most breakdowns occur (we have cited extensive evidence on the root causes of stall-outs from our own research and from others throughout this book, with the conclusion that the root cause is most often internal and most often related to failure to achieve full potential in the core). The ability to execute this middle-area strategy well is the mainspring of successful repeatable models.

Some areas outside of business, such as the military, have a longer history of using nonnegotiables in creating consistent behavior across a theater of combat while not overly constraining the ability to respond to unique conditions on the ground. This idea is called *commander's intent.*

Commander's Intent

Commander's intent refers to a small number of simple statements that outline the purpose of a mission and the key principles that must be followed. Commander's intent is a way to coordinate many groups and functions during the fog of a complex combat operation. According to military doctrine, the statements are written for at least two levels below the "commander."

This concept originated to connect centralized strategy with the decentralized, and often completely isolated, pockets of combat forces. For instance, Napoleon "developed an organizational method—the Corps d'Armée system—to reduce the uncertainty and complexity inherent in battle . . . by decentralizing the system, Napoleon was able to decrease the number of translations that orders went through. This structure revolutionized command systems, and armies were thereafter thought of more as collectives of distributed missions that contributed to a common goal."[4] Today, with the extraordinarily rapid pace of events in military theaters, commander's intent has become an even more critical part of military doctrine: "The commander's intent is a clear, concise statement of what the force must do and the conditions the force must establish with respect to the enemy, terrain, and civil considerations that represent the desired end state."[5]

Since 1990, the U.S. military has made a substantial push to refine commander's intent, as the advent of laser-guided ordnance, satellites, drones, and wireless computers at the front line has compressed time to almost a point of instant response. Under these conditions, the view of famous general Helmuth von Moltke that "no battle plan survives the first contact with the enemy" becomes even truer.

Nonnegotiables are the business equivalent of commander's intent.

Why Is Commander's Intent So Hard to Implement in Business?

On the one hand, all of this could sound simple—"How can it be that hard to align the front line around the core ideas of the business, the same as the management team?" Yet, for some reason, it does not happen in business as much as it should. We have identified some of the key obstacles that seem to get in the way of shortening the effective distance between management and the front line that is serving the customer:

- "The customer is a number, not a person." Insulated by phone menu options and distant call centers, senior management can easily spend less and less time interacting with customers, and especially ultimate end users (when products are sold through channels). In the best businesses, we find that senior managers spend at least one-third of their time with customers; in most businesses, it is a much smaller number. New technologies should make this easier to do, yet ironically they can also create a layer of insulation, contributing to a false sense of customer intimacy. This can drive a huge wedge between the front line and management.

- "The thin blue line of customer care." When customer care and after-service is viewed as an expense to be managed down (as it is in many businesses; we know one company that would shut down the free 1-800 number for customer service in order to save money), you have a problem. The principles underlying the Great Repeatable Models are meant to reduce the odds of mortgaging the future by liquidating customer goodwill at a discount.

- "Sales are the other guys." Some businesses have cultures that devalue the sales and service roles, as opposed to exalting it as the eyes and ears on the ground, as the intelligence function about customer needs and competitive offerings.

- "Tyranny of functions." In some companies, internal functions become service centers for other internal customers, creating an entire internal ecosystem with a life of its own independent of the customer and the value that these functions actually create that the customer would pay for. If you are having too many internal meetings, and if this accounts for more than 10 percent of your time, then you might have this problem.

- "Myth of stakeholder priorities." When customers become one of a long list of stakeholders in the queue of competing company priorities (rather than having the highest and unique position), customers can become undervalued, and the gap between senior management's mentality and the market reality at the front line increases.

- "Layered organizational complexity." Organizations add complexity when they grow, especially in the absence of a repeatable formula. We conducted a survey of executives and found that 68 percent felt that adjacency moves in pursuit of growth proved "much more complex" than they had originally anticipated.[6] The easy short-term path is then to layer systems and coordinating functions on top of that to keep track of or manage the complexity they have wrought through expansion. Addressing complexity with more complexity has the effect over time of disconnecting top management from the front line and turning major decisions into a fuzz ball of committees where no one really knows who decides. This is how complexity kills speed, responsiveness, and ultimately growth.

What Makes a Good Nonnegotiable?

The most valuable nonnegotiables are hard and serious, not soft and fuzzy. They change behavior, affect decisions, define rewards, shape culture, and even guide recruitment. Certainly, you can find lists all over the place in business that masquerade as core principles. Even Enron—perhaps the most vilified company of its generation—claimed to have statements of values, including phrases like these: "We treat others as we would like to be treated ourselves . . . we do not tolerate abusive or disrespectful treatment. Ruthlessness, callousness, and arrogance don't belong here."[7] But these imposters are not what we are talking about. So how can you make sure that your nonnegotiables are not ineffective, and even ironic, like those at Enron? Here are seven characteristics of effective nonnegotiables.

Connect to Frontline Actions

The most important pillars of your strategy obviously need to be hardwired to frontline behaviors and even out to the customer. Without this wiring, they remain at the level of public relations phrases and wall plaques that gather dust. With it, a CEO can reduce the distance between management and frontline employees, and increase self-organizing behaviors.

Despite the poor returns in the past twenty years of the global auto industry, Toyota has marched steadily to leadership, with 7 percent revenue and profit growth, and 9 percent total annual shareholder returns over the twenty-five years up to the financial crisis. Central to the Toyota system are fourteen Toyota Way principles, tracing back to the founder, that shape not only specific details of the Toyota Production System, but also its culture.[8] Toyota has even allowed its competitors to visit its plants and study its system, secure in the knowledge they could not replicate its success.

Steven Spear and Kent Bowen conducted a four-year study of the Toyota Production System across forty plants in the United States, Europe, and Japan. Their conclusions reinforce the link between nonnegotiable principles and an effective repeatable model in business:

> So, why has it been so difficult to decode the Toyota Production System? The answer, we believe, is that observers confuse the tools and practices they see on their plant visits with the system itself. That makes it impossible for them to resolve the apparent paradox of the system—namely, that activities, connections, and production flows in a Toyota factory are rigorously scripted, yet at the same time Toyota's operations are enormously flexible and adaptable. Activities and processes are constantly being challenged and pushed to higher levels of performance, enabling the company to continually innovate and improve. To understand Toyota's success, you have to unravel the paradox—you have to see that the rigid specification is the very thing that makes the flexibility and creativity possible.[9]

They go on to say, about the "rules and principles" that have evolved over fifty years, "We describe four principles—three rules of design, which show how Toyota sets up all its operations as experiments, and one rule of improvement, which describes how Toyota teaches the scientific method to workers at every level of the organization. It is these rules—and not the specific practices and tools that people observe during their plant visits—that in our opinion form the essence of Toyota's system. That is why we think of the rules as the DNA of the Toyota Production System."[10]

The first rule of the system is that every repetitive activity be studied and specified in its best practice. Even seat installation is specified down to the order of the bolts, how to tighten them, and the required torque, until the moment that a better way is found. Not much is more core to Toyota than car assembly, so it is entirely appropriate that such learning is tightly codified, versus practices in less core areas that would just create bureaucracy.

Affect Trade-offs with Real Economic Consequences

A nonnegotiable is most valuable when it helps with difficult decisions. Sometimes it does so by prohibiting certain types of behavior (e.g., at Vanguard—"We will not pay for distribution of our products") and sometimes by demanding certain types of behaviors. As Vanguard CEO Bill McNabb commented to us, "Some of the greatest benefits from our core principles are seen in the difficult decisions where we decide not to do something as a result. Often the things you say no to turn out to be among the most important choices, and our core principles help us to do that."[11]

One of Vanguard's nonnegotiables is to focus on long-term, loyal individual investors above all else. This was tested when a large investor wanted to put $40 million into a Vanguard short-term treasury debt fund for only six to eight weeks, creating two transaction fees essentially to "park" the money in a fund of $430 million, where this large transaction cost could affect other investors. Vanguard turned down the check and the customer, saying that it would not let its loyal customers subsidize the "hot money" costs of short-term investors. That is a nonnegotiable in action.

Reinforce the Strongest Competitive Advantage

The mantra at Tetra Pak that the "package must save more than it costs" stems from its founder and was the original reason for developing the tetrahedron-shaped package for milk. Today, that principle lives on at Tetra Pak and is a standard that every major new product and innovation, from new package designs to new lines of equipment, must meet. Tetra Pak has developed sophisticated methods to evaluate the systems cost of packaging, from production cost to spoilage (a strength of a Tetra Pak for ambient milk), to transportation and storage (Tetra Paks are designed to optimize on truck and shelf efficiency), to disposal costs. Tetra Pak's Operational Cost Reduction program claims that it can go into the typical dairy or juicer and reduce operating costs by as much as 12 percent. This mantra that Tetra Pak must essentially fully pay for itself through the efficiencies that it creates for the customer is a powerful nonnegotiable.

Can Be Reapplied in New Markets

The more readily that a nonnegotiable can be applied to new markets, the greater its value. A nonnegotiable of Olam's strategy, and a key source of competitive advantage, is the insistence that its supply chain extend right up to the farm gate. Most of the "profit pool" in the commodities that Olam distributes occurs from the farm to the dock, so the more you tap into it, the more you can capitalize on the full economics. Much of the most powerful information for risk management originates with each farmer, so this direct contact yields better intelligence and better ability to respond. Building farmer relationships is a built-in stabilizer for sudden price surges or changes in conditions. As articulated earlier, this nonnegotiable translates into specific local behaviors, from recruiting to an ethos of focusing on the farmer and the farming community. One manager told us how he drove a family member of the local police chief to work for six weeks when the family had problems with transport. This principle, central to Olam's competitive advantage, is nonnegotiable across its two hundred product–market combinations.

Link to rewards and deeper sources of motivation

Enterprise Rent-A-Car is the largest car rental company in the world. It has the largest fleet of cars in the United States and is America's largest hirer of college graduates—all on the back of thirty years of sustained and profitable growth. Central to its operating principles is customer loyalty. As CEO Andy Taylor says, "The only way to grow is to treat customers so well they come back for more and tell their friends about us. Golden Rule behavior is the basis for loyalty. And loyalty is the key to profitable growth."[12]

This nonnegotiable to put customer loyalty above all else is reinforced through a measurement system based on asking renters the single question about whether they were completely satisfied with their rental. The company compiles the "top box" scores—completely satisfied—into what it calls the Enterprise Service Quality Index (ESQi). This measure of loyalty is published for its seventy-six hundred rental locations. Branches that score below average are not allowed to have any members of their team promoted. Some teams have gone so far as to rank customer-friendly behaviors of every individual within their branch. Where they have done this, the accountability and reward system lead to higher scores—and, of course, more promotions.

Are Mutually Reinforcing

The nonnegotiables should reinforce each other. They are not meant to be just a series of sensible but independent propositions. For instance, the elegance of the Danaher Business System (DBS) lies in the way it creates a comprehensive and internally consistent way to manage industrial and medical technology businesses, with core principles tracing back to its modified version of the Toyota Production System but applied to all core processes in the company. DBS creates a consistent language and lens on business that can be applied from shop floor operations to sales force optimization—a mutually reinforcing system.

Liberate Positive Energy

Nonnegotiables reinforce what is special about a company and can even be a source of pride for its employees. They are a key method by which the CEO and the front line can compress the distance between each other. Just consider this statement of Apple's core values, a high-level form of nonnegotiable in that company:[13]

- We believe that we are on the face of the earth to make great products.

- We constantly focus on innovation.

- We believe in the simple, not the complex.

- We believe that we need to own and control the primary technologies behind the products that we make.

- We participate only in markets where we can make a significant contribution.

- We believe in saying no to thousands of projects so that we can really focus on the few that are truly important and meaningful to us.

- We believe in deep collaboration and cross pollination of our groups, which allow us to innovate in a way that others cannot.

- We don't settle for anything less than excellence.

- We have the self-honesty to admit when we're wrong and the courage to change.

That's pretty motivating.

One CEO commented on how nonnegotiables can do this:

> We wanted to develop a principle around always delivering superior products. This led to a huge debate about how to test for superiority. There were different issues. First, do we do "blind testing" or not? The second was on which attributes did we need to test superior? We found the easy part of creating the nonnegotiable was the "what"—of course we wanted to only release better products. The hard conversations were around those two issues. We finally agreed that the nonnegotiable would be, "All new innovations must be superior, as measured through blind testing against the most important preference drivers of the target customer." It is a mouthful, but that single phrase has stopped hours and hours of debates that have been going on for at least a decade.

The System: From Strategy to Nonnegotiables to Daily Routines

The systematic translation of strategy into a set of commonly shared principles that ultimately drives more self-organizing behaviors and decisions at the front line is what we refer to as *freedom in a framework* (see figure 3-2). This diagram illustrates the five levels that need to be well defined, highly tangible, and consistent and that we discuss in this chapter. Some of the Great Repeatable Model companies we examined blend together core values and the nonnegotiables; others might articulate the essence of the strategy in the simplest of terms, choosing to push more detail into the nonnegotiable principles and routines. However, the best ones all did these five things visibly, albeit in their own ways.

FIGURE 3-2

Nonnegotiables translate the strategy for the front line

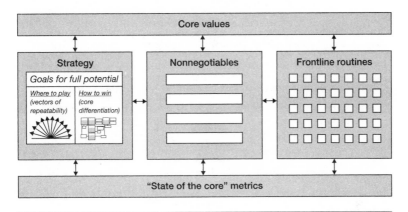

Let's return to IKEA to illustrate how this might work. Start with the statements that define the purpose of IKEA and its core values from founder Ingvar Kamprad from his thesis "Testament of a Furniture Dealer." Principle 4 is, "Reach good results with small means. Expensive solutions are often a sign of mediocrity. We have no interest in a solution until we know what it costs."[14] This fundamental tenet of the strategy, a statement of a deeply embedded business principle, then translates in practice into the nonnegotiables of the organization, such as an insistence on designing to a price point and a relentless cost focus on every detail of design.

How this translates further into specific routines and behaviors is illustrated by the case of the Bang mug. IKEA decided in 1996 to create a mug that could be sold for only five Swedish kronor (about fifty cents at the time). The company decided to avoid red pigments because they were more costly than yellow, green, and blue. Due to the cost focus, a design requirement was to maximize the number of mugs that could be stored on a pallet. "Originally 864 mugs would fit, after the redesign with a rim, 1280 and after another redesign 2024. This allowed shipping cost to be reduced by 60%."[15] The next-generation version of the mug was further redesigned so that more could fit into the kiln in manufacturing, further shaving the cost. Even in this simple example of a fifty-cent basic mug, you can see the sequence at work from principle to strategy, to nonnegotiable, to detailed routines. This depth is why IKEA is so difficult to emulate, despite the apparent obviousness of the concept.

We turn now, briefly, to comment on the three areas in figure 3-2 that shape, surround, and support the nonnegotiables in their central position on the business model stage. These are (1) the importance of a small number of deep, core routines by which the most essential purpose of the nonnegotiables is enforced, (2) a small set of "state of the core" metrics that represent the bellwether of a business, and (3) higher-level principles and beliefs, often tracing back to the founder and providing an enormous sense of history and stability for Great Repeatable Model companies.

Deeper Impact: Embedded Routines

From the way professional tennis players prepare for big matches to the business processes around product feedback in an Apple store, some of the most consistent behaviors often turn into routines. Ultimately, the nonnegotiables must be embedded into the most important core processes that drive the business.

The story of the creation of the largest beer company in the world, AB InBev, illustrates the origins and ultimate competitive power of such routines. In 1999, Interbrew, the foundation for what is now AB InBev, was a regional beer company with more than 50 percent revenue coming from European operations, totaling 3.2 billion euros in revenues, with about 16 percent operating profit margin. Today, following the mergers with Ambev, the leader in South America in 2004, and with Anheuser-Busch, the leader in the United States in 2008, the company has grown by eight times and increased its operating profit margin to an industry best of 31 percent while becoming the world leader in beer—about 40 percent larger than its nearest competitor.

The success of AB InBev has been its ability to build leadership positions in its major brand and geography combinations and to be the low-cost producer in most of those markets. The engine of the approach to becoming the world's lowest-cost beer company is a set of three repeatable systems, called WCCP (world-class customer processes), VPO (Voyager Plant Optimization), and ZBB (zero-based budget process).

Take ZBB, for instance, to see how a set of nonnegotiables (low-cost-producer status, pursuit of best practices, treating expense money as your own, and always zero basing expense levels) is driven into frontline routines, in one element of cost such as travel and expenses. This is one of sixteen "packages" of cost that the nonmanufacturing part of the P&L statement is divided into. Each of the packages has a global "owner" at the management level as well as regional owners. They are charged with driving a well-defined process each year to set benchmark targets, zero base these parts of the budgets, identify best practices to become more cost effective, create completely transparent metrics across the company, and be part of the ZBB team to communicate these globally.

Most of these nonnegotiables and routines trace their roots to earlier years—as is so often the case. In this instance, many of these practices originated with the founders of Ambev, which was one of the great business success stories in South America at the time it combined with Interbrew. Ambev transformed itself from a marginally profitable company with a high cost structure acquired by a private equity firm in the 1980s to a highly profitable business with more than 70 percent of the Brazilian beer market and low-cost-producer status across South America. Ambev acquired and improved brewers throughout South America using its repeatable model. After the merger, the system was extended globally and further codified in the form of these three cost-oriented programs—the epicenter of the company's strategy and differentiation. These repeatable routines were introduced into Anheuser-Busch, providing a key reason why AB InBev is on target for aggressive postmerger cost improvements.

Routines are the "habits" of an organization. Yet, as with people, these are not easy to change. For instance, only one person in seven after a heart attack actually makes a lasting change in diet, exercise, or lifestyle. The average person makes the same New Year's resolution ten times in a row without lasting change. No wonder that more than 70 percent of organizational change initiatives in companies fail completely.[16] This is why change programs need to take special care to be highly specific and to focus energy on those most critical routines that need to change, and to persist in driving that change through deeply.

"State-of-the-Core" Metrics

Parallel to the nonnegotiable principles in Great Repeatable Model companies were usually an equally small number of state-of-the-core measures of the health of the core model with relevance down to the front line of the company.

Peter Drucker has also emphasized this point throughout his writings: "I have found it practicable and effective to provide even a foreman with a detailed statement of not only his own objectives, but those of the company . . . Even though the company is so large as to make the distance between the individual foreman's production and the company's total output all but astronomical, the result has been a significant increase in production. Indeed, this must follow if we mean it when we say that the foreman is part of management. For it is the definition of a manager that in what he does he takes responsibility for the whole—that, in cutting stone, he 'builds the cathedral.'"[17]

Dell created one of the greatest repeatable formulas in business during the 1990s, when Dell was the best-performing large company stock in the world for a decade. Though failure to adapt has befallen the company during the following decade, there are still lessons to learn from the breathtaking speed of global deployment of the Dell model, and the use of a few state-of-the-core metrics to drive behavior and consistent focus. When Dell was entering a key stage of its growth— designing its model to reproduce and adapt the formula to other countries (starting with the six major markets), to other products (from personal computers to servers and beyond), and to other segments (from business to consumer, to education, to government, etc.)—the management team did something that proved to be extremely insightful. It decided to highlight massively at all levels of the organization (including extensive bonus linkages) a small number of physical measures—different from the normal accounting numbers—that represented the state of the core, the deep health of the direct model.

There were five such measures, and everyone knew them. Two related to product failure rates and incidences of successful repair. One was product fill rate—ship to order. So, three were directly focused on the customer experience, which, at the time, was one of the great advantages of the direct (speaking directly to customers and shipping directly to customers) model. The others were the cash conversion cycle (a measure of the inventory and velocity through the supply chain) and growth relative to the market. During that period of explosive growth and profitability, these measures were central to every product, geography, and segment review as the company grew along these three vectors, constantly cloning and adapting to new segments and markets.

Our two hundred–company database probed such simple state-of-the-core metrics. We asked, (1) Is the business managed with a few, specially well-recognized key metrics that stand out above the others? (2) Is the state of the core monitored with a simple dashboard? (3) Are these most important metrics visible and cascaded down the organization? and (4) Do changes in these metrics drive strong actions and decisions? We found strong relationships between the best-performing companies and the clarity and simplicity of the metrics. The best performers, on the 5-point scale for each question, were rated nearly a point higher, on average.

The Role of Core Values and Beliefs

Nonnegotiables are always informed, even driven, by some strongly held basic assumptions about how the world works and what it means to do well. This was seen in our database analysis as well as in our case examples—where virtually all thirty of the repeatable models we looked at most closely had some form of prominent core values and beliefs. In many instances, these core values are the "tablets from the mount" of a company, often tracing back to the founder and refined by later generations (IKEA, Vanguard, Tetra Pak, MSC Industrial Supply Company, and LEGO are a few of the examples in this book that illustrate this pattern). Though, sometimes, they emerge later

(NIKE, DaVita, and AmBev are examples of this). Consider, for instance, the NIKE maxims.

The NIKE Maxims

NIKE has transformed a low-growth business of rubber-soled shoes (sneakers) into a high-performance, high-margin business built around the marquee athletes of the world. NIKE has gone from strength to strength for four decades, changing continuously in a dynamic industry (just think of how much the businesses of sports, new materials, media, and channels have changed during that time!). During its history, NIKE has experienced a couple of periods of stall-out, yet each time it was able to regain its momentum by innovating around its business model, increasing its organizational capacity, and building always around the core principles that have made it special—an effective blend of constant change and relatively stable principles.

Part of NIKE's "special sauce" includes eleven maxims that define the company's point of view on its business and reinforce desired behaviors. Such codification is especially vital in geographies like Korea or Australia that are distant from the original home market. For instance, in July 2010, NIKE Australia held a "maxim award" day to celebrate individual employees who personified each of the eleven maxims. The awards were given out by iconic Australian athletes.

The maxims are summarized in table 3-1. Maxim 4, for instance, is "Simplify and Go" (described in much more detail in the NIKE handbook). It is focused on increasing speed, and reducing fear of taking risk and making mistakes. Maxim 9 is "Master the Fundamentals." These maxims combine a belief system about business in general (e.g., maxim 9) with a set of principles about the drivers of its specific business (e.g., maxim 3: "NIKE is a Brand").

TABLE 3-1

NIKE's eleven maxims

It is our nature to innovate	Think something nobody else thinks, build something nobody else builds, or improve something that already exists. Lighter, faster, stronger, bigger, smaller, funnier. Make it great. This is what we do best.
NIKE is a company	We call it NIKE, Inc., and it lives in many worlds: product, sports, media, entertainment, lifestyle, and retail. Our position allows us to lead in all of these areas.
NIKE is a brand	We call it the Swoosh. Little wing. Inspired by the Greek goddess of victory, that simple checkmark is the symbol of global leadership in sports products and attitude. The NIKE brand is our incubator for great research, design, and development.
Simplify and go	Life is too short and the competition too fast to spend time in pointless debate and gratuitous nuance. The more honest and clear we are with each other, the faster we move and the better we work.
The consumer decides	To reach consumers, we maintain wide-open dialogue, sharing ideas and insights back and forth to understand the infinite variety of their cultural views, and to assure that they understand NIKE. The day you take consumers for granted is the day they leave you.
Be a sponge	Curiosity is life. Assumption is death. Look around. Open your heart and mind, and you open the future. There are great ideas lying around like diamonds in the dirt. The brightest are those you see out of the corner of your eye.
Evolve immediately	NIKE takes the glacial view of evolution and puts a blowtorch to it. We amplify what's good and change what isn't. We are in perpetual motion. We like success. We love momentum. We are best when we are lean and fast. Add to the never-ending NIKE story.
Do the right thing	Embrace the truth. Be transparent. Seek diversity. Promote sustainability. These values are a part of who we are. Our success depends on it.
Master the fundamentals	There is no substitute for doing the hard work first. The commitment to excel and an unwavering focus on process are at the root of superior performance. Lance Armstrong knows it.

We are on the offense. Always.	Our job is to stay aggressive and committed to a game plan of our own design. We influence. We lead. If we can't lead it, we don't need it.
Remember the man	His name is Bowerman. It's German for "builder man." He did more to shape athletics and NIKE around the world than any three people combined. His spirit still blows change into every corner of NIKE.

Note: Descriptions of the maxims have been condensed but use the original wording.
Source: Company materials.

Reflecting on the practical use of these maxims, Charlie Denson, president of NIKE Brand, told us:[18]

> Mark [President and CEO Mark Parker] and I created the Nike Maxims in 2000. 1997–2000 had been a rough period for NIKE. Revenues had stalled out a bit, and it was a slow period for the brand and the company—a swoon, not a swoosh. We realized that we had hit a new level of size and maturity and had outgrown some of the more informal processes of the past. So we revised the mission statement, formalized the three axes of geography, product, and segment that we would measure and run the company on and developed the maxims to energize and align our increasingly complex organization.
>
> The maxims had been written down in different ways over the years, and the ideas really stemmed back to the founders and especially Phil Knight, as an embodiment of many aspects of his personality, from teamwork to intense competitiveness. We felt that we had lost some of the culture of the past, that it had become diluted, and we had to go back to a purer version of the things the company stood for stated in a more contemporary manner. We then, with Phil, flew around the world and discussed them with every employee for a couple of days in each session. We provided conclusive stories of

each, often with people involved in the stories talking about them. We emphasized how they define NIKE and shape our behaviors.

We were amazed by the power of the maxims. They started showing up the next day all over the place and it has continued. We reference them a lot, and they guide us during difficult decisions and trying times. Though we give awards in regions, business areas, and globally for each maxim, we have tried to leave aspects a bit intangible because we feel there is a level of interpretation that changes and makes them more sustainable than if they were too rigid.

We look on ourselves as a company that adapts fast and reinvents itself every ninety days, so that balance of flexibility in the business model with clarity around what really is our core has been essential for us. Looking back, they were absolutely central to the revitalization of the company since 2000, and our ability to drive through the $18 billion revenue mark.

Organizations with a proven ability to endure and to replicate successfully almost always, it seemed, used the power of principles. Virtually all of our Great Repeatable Model case studies, we found, contained a clear belief system that shaped the "soul" of the company. We also found such belief systems in enduring nonbusiness institutions. For instance, The Salvation Army, started in 1865, is one of the most beloved charitable institutions in America, and now encompasses more than 104,000 employees in 124 countries, supported by 3.4 million volunteers. Central to the organization are the eleven doctrines defining the core beliefs of its members' battle against social distress. Or take the Olympics, often at the center of political currents among its participating countries. Yet, the Games' integrity has been able to endure, in part, through the set of agreed principles at the core of the Olympic Games, like the Olympic creed, the Olympic oath, and the three values of the Olympics.

Back to another business example to close this discussion of the power of principles. MSC is the leader in a relatively nonexotic business: the distribution of supplies for the metalworking industry. Its history shows how the elements of the original repeatable model and the core values that helped to differentiate it not only fueled the early phase of its growth, but also were rediscovered in a new light by the son of the founder, who used them to renew growth. It is a testament to the role of principles in the Great Repeatable Models.

MSC: The Power of Principles in the Evolution of a Business Model

The power of deep-seated values and beliefs is sometimes a hidden asset waiting to be discovered and utilized—a thread of constancy through the evolution of a business model. An example of this is the history of MSC, a seventy-year-old distributor of industrial supplies that has achieved sustained value creator performance (ninefold growth in just fourteen years in a low-growth industry), which would put it into the top 5 percent of companies worldwide. The story of its persistence (always profitable) and growth (acceleration around having the elements of a repeatable model come together later in its life cycle) shows the power of principles in sustaining repeatable models.

Mitchell Jacobson, chairman, son of the founder, and former CEO of MSC Industrial Supply Company, sat back against a wall containing the first financial statement of the company in a letter to his father. We had asked him about the evolution of the business that was started by Sid Jacobson as Sid Tool company in 1941. We were especially interested in the company's historical pattern—always profitable—but with a five-decade-long ramp-up to $175 million in 1994 and then a rapid acceleration in just a decade and a half (in a very low-growth market) to $1.5 billion in 2009. What changed? What decisions were made? Where did the repeatable model come in? How did it build on the principles of the past?

Mitchell Jacobson responded:

> A company is not so different from people. Think of a company in terms of its life cycle. It starts like a baby kicking and screaming and moving around. If you figure out what works, then it starts to grow up. It then becomes a teenager with tremendous hubris and gets in trouble, but learns life lessons. At last it becomes an adult with wisdom, but hopefully still has a sense of adventure and excitement. Some companies grow old, with tired board rooms and somber pictures of past CEOs peering down, but our goal as the company has grown up has been to keep it young and innovative, blending the strong core beliefs that have proven relevant at every stage of the life cycle with constant renewal and new ways to differentiate in how we serve customers. Of course, the baby and the innovator stage is about my dad. He started the company as a kid during the Depression who was not able to finish high school because he had to go right to work and support the family.
>
> My dad started the company in Lower Manhattan, selling supplies to tool companies. When he left with his brother to fight in World War II, their sisters took over and kept it going. They returned in 1945 and realized that, as veterans, they were allowed to buy war supplies in large amounts, and began making bulk purchases, breaking it down, and supplying local companies. Later, he was on vacation in California and saw

a catalog for Marshall Tool & Supply. He learned how it worked and decided to transfer the idea to the East Coast as a way to diversify and, ultimately, as the new core of the company. He would literally sell during the day and sit at home after dinner and paste together the catalog himself.[19]

Fast-forward to 1994. Mitchell, the son, is now CEO. Revenues are $175 million. The catalog has been successful up and down the eastern seaboard, and a few local offices have been opened to support sales. But what next? Was it possible and valuable, the team asked, to try to increase the company by a factor of five or ten times? Was the current model scalable? Was there a source of differentiation in the use of the catalog combined with their practices of customer focus, which they believed were an advantage in the market? Could they repeat it?

"So, we decided to move into adjacent categories in our catalog and to start to build out the national footprint of 500,000 items in stock, distribution centers and branches. To fund it, we took the company public in 1995. This was a dream for my father, a Depression kid now buying the first one hundred shares of his company on the New York Stock Exchange. But, without fully realizing it at the time, we were in the process of stumbling over the elements of the next version of a repeatable formula that we could apply nationally," Jacobson said.[20] It proved to be a blend of the old model (focus on metalworking supplies, and the central role of the catalog), original core values (egalitarianism, customer focus as a competitive advantage, and high ethics), and some new elements (local sales offices, product expansion into adjacent segments to fill out the catalog). The values, though, especially persisted and became even more important in an increasingly large business. Jacobson explained:

For instance, we all have the same size offices, no
designated parking spots other than one reserved in
the name of Sid, and we collect feedback from various
levels of the company that interact with a new recruit—
not just the managers doing the interviews—on their
perception of people who want to work here. These
routines reinforce our repeatable model. We believe
that the person on the front line must take care of the
customer and have wide parameters of action, but with
clear principles and rules that we all share. We never
want people to say, "I have to check with a manager,"
when they are serving customers. We conduct focus
groups with our front line associates to get honest
feedback about how we're doing, without their super-
visor in the room. We think this culture is core to our
differentiation.[21]

The expansion launched by Jacobson was mostly organic,
though it included some acquisitions, culminating in 2006 with
the acquisition of the company's largest, focused metalworking
supply competitor, called J&L. This expansion strategy, from
the 1995 IPO to 2008, the completion of the J&L integration,
showed excellent results—growth in revenues of 16 percent
per year, in earnings of 18 percent, and in free cash flow of
18 percent, leading to return on invested capital of 20 percent
at the end of the period, and a stock price that had increased by
nearly four times.

Current CEO David Sandler explained what he referred to
as "the constants of our repeatable model, which we found
consistent with the thinking of everyone we met at the company
at all levels: (1) a culture of winning and empowering associates.
Our egalitarianism and trust of the front line is absolutely essential to our differentiation; we believe in openness and 'no place

to hide' if we really need to get something done that is meaningful; (2) customer focus and a high service model that gives our front line the power to act; (3) a core focused around unplanned purchases and the metalworking industry, where we are now the clear national leader; (4) a constant stream of adjacency expansions to replicate and refine the model in new areas; (5) a set of coherent core values that go back to Sid Jacobson, our founder; and (6) a set of ways that we get feedback from the front line directly to our managers." One talk Sandler gives to his employees, or as MSC calls its team, "associates" starts by saying, "I thought it would be helpful to talk a bit about an important part of our culture—our core values and how we do business. Regardless of the economic climate, whether in slow times or high-growth periods, regardless of what is currently in vogue or the latest in business trends, we operate with a core set of principles that began going all the way back to our founding by Sid Jacobson in 1941."[22]

We shift now to the amazing story of the turnaround of DaVita. It shows how one management team, facing bankruptcy of their core, remade the core principles and nonnegotiables of the business, moving the company from the worst performer in the industry to the best.

DaVita: Renewal through repeatability

When Kent Thiry took the helm as CEO of Total Renal Care in 1999, the status of the company and its 460 renal dialysis centers was in doubt. It was losing more than $60 million per year, was under investigation for fraud by the federal government, had a 40 percent turnover of staff per year, and exhibited poor clinical outcome measures relative to its peers (see table 3-2). Its bank covenants had been broken by this performance, and the company was hurtling toward bankruptcy and worried about meeting its payroll. In less than twenty-four months, the

TABLE 3-2

DaVita's before and after statistics

		Total Renal Care (1999)	DaVita (2010)
Financials	Revenue	$1.2B	$6.4B
	Operating income	-$60M	$997M
	Market share	12%	30%
Patients and community	Mortality rate	>20%	<16%
	Clinical outcomes	Average	Materially better than industry
	Community programs	0	>20
Teammates	Job perception	Just a job	Truly caring community
	Employee turnover	40%	18%
	Employee productivity	Average	10% improvement

Source: Comapay data.

share price had declined from $23.00 per share to $1.71 and was threatening to head even lower. The structure of the business was a model of nonrepeatability. As Thiry said, "We had 460 centers operating in 460 completely separate ways."[23]

The first four priorities in the turnaround were to collect cash (bills were taking more than two weeks to send out, and that was cut to two days, for instance) and stabilize the balance sheet, to build a completely new management team, to make progress and create credibility with investors and employees, and, interestingly, to create a shared vision of the future that was motivating and worth pursuing.

In a move that most would not make at a time of crisis (and that surprised many in the company), CEO Thiry decided to spend the time and money to hold a meeting in Phoenix, Arizona, of the top seven hundred people in the company. The purpose was to define an elevating mission and vision to pursue, and to kick off a year-long process of defining the values that the employees wanted the company to stand for and insist on. Of this time, Thiry told us:

> Ten years ago the company had totally imploded and suffered a $23.00 to $1.71 stock price decline. It had lost any sense of soul. Debt payments were behind. Employees were alienated. Executives were leaving left and right. The company was being investigated by the SEC. Nonetheless, early on, the new team made a decision to be a community first and a company second. A community that happens to be organized in terms of a company.
>
> Think of a small town where people have to pay taxes, this is OK if people feel they get value, a good police force, roads, parks. Similarly there is no problem with shareholder profit in return for capital put into the business as long as the right things are done for the patients and teammates. But it must be fair and transparent.
>
> Some of the board of directors were afraid that this community philosophy (including calling the CEO a "mayor") would lead people to take advantage of us. We have found reality to be quite the opposite. We have found that even though 90 percent of our 16,000 technicians did not go to college, they totally understand the importance of profit. We are the only *Fortune* 500 company where the people chose the name and logo of the company and chose the core values in a seven-month process. There were a couple of thousand teammates involved.

Many people would have advised leaving these "softer issues" of values and principles until the company was stabilized financially, but Thiry and his management team felt differently. They were proved right. Since the program to define the mission and core values (and company name) was initiated, the stock price has increased from $1.71 to more than $70 per share, and earnings have grown from a $67 million loss to a profit (EBIT) of $947 million. At the same time, DaVita's market share in the United States has increased from 12 percent to 30 percent (see table 3-2). From near bankruptcy, DaVita (the name chosen by employees, meaning "giving life") has put together a ten-year run that places it solidly in our category of the 10 percent of global companies that are sustained value creators, based on its growth and returns. From a nadir of employee morale, DaVita has even made its way onto *Fortune*'s World's Most Admired Companies list.

The seven values chosen by the employees through many interactive sessions are service excellence, integrity, team, continuous improvement, accountability, fulfillment, and fun. Each of these values cascades down into behaviors and further specifics. At the time, the company had severe problems along many of these fundamental dimensions. Services were below industry standard. The team fabric was in disrepair. There was no continuous improvement or learning, as the business information was not transparent and the centers' operations were not repeatable or standardized in any way. Accountability was often unclear. No one felt fulfilled, nor were they having fun.

The company began to create ways to reinforce and reward these values. DaVita established DaVita Academy and University to teach a more repeatable approach to the business and to reinforce these values with tools to accomplish them. A series of town hall meetings was started to bring the front line in frequent contact with top management. A "DaVita way of managing" began to be developed. To bind the front line even more tightly with management, the organization was designed to be flatter, and Kent Thiry began answering directly hundreds of e-mails from employees all over the company, further compressing the distance from the CEO to the front line.

The core values were made central to hiring criteria, and team members were given an evaluation form to provide input on whether they felt every hiring candidate would stack up on these values. Annual reviews and 360-degree feedback mechanics were put in place, built heavily around behaviors to reinforce the company's mission and the values. Patients filled out cards for caregivers they felt fulfilled these values, and awards were given at each branch (scholarships for children, paid vacations, best parking spots, etc.), where all the patient cards were read out loud for winners.

Metrics followed next. Working closely with the front line, DaVita created state-of-the-core metrics at the level of each center, aggregated to each region, and for the whole company. One, called the DaVita Quality Index (DQI), is a measure of clinical outcomes across seven health indications.

Thiry commented on the power of a few, focused metrics:

> This is a fascinating one, where we have traveled a bit of a journey, one that is absolutely central to creating the kind of repeatable model that we needed. There are so many possible measures in our business that it is easy to lose track. We came up with the DaVita Quality Index that combines measures for patients in our own creative way and translates it all into a number of points. Every center knows its own DQI score and how it compares to others'. It is not perfect, but we want frontline people to take real pride in getting the number up. And they can't do that if there are thirteen numbers. Now I have people come up to me and say with real excitement and pride, "We are now in the top half in DQI." We even tie bonuses to it. Even more important, we now have a growing body of evidence showing a strong correlation between DQI and lower patient mortality.[24]

DaVita's mission is to be the "provider, partner and employer of choice" in its industry. A key principle in support of this mission is around the clinical results and customer experience of the patient, expressed as "Patient Quality of Life Equals Job 1." This high-level principle is then implemented through a series of nonnegotiables that influence the choices and decisions at the front line of patient care. One is "No backward integration." Though DaVita's competitors earn profits by producing or sourcing their own proprietary supplies, DaVita has decided that it is best to comb the industry for best-in-class products and go with those. This is a nonnegotiable. Another is to always strive to "Surround the patient with value-added services." DaVita believes that it creates better care for the patient, a better customer experience, and a superior business by investing heavily in the value-added services that surround the patient beyond dialysis itself. This includes a focused renal pharmacy, vascular access centers, and a unique approach to coordinating all care services called VillageHealth. The kidney-care pharmacy usage can, DaVita has found, drive 82 percent higher adherence to medication regimens, which is above the industry average of approximately 45 percent. This is an example of how a high-level mission can translate to the front line and measurable patient outcomes through a version of nonnegotiables.

Thiry reflected on the transformation: "I realized that many corporations are lifeless, emotionally sterile, and culturally empty despite the fact that people spend a lot of their life in them. This was especially critical to address given how decentralized our teammates are, how pressurized their work is helping patients with renal failure, and how easy it is to create a gap between management and the people at the front lines, and that was something I felt had to be addressed to have a sustainable strategy for DaVita. Equally important, it is just a better way to live."[25]

DaVita became strong enough to go on the acquisition trail, purchasing Gambro's 564 outpatient dialysis centers in the United States with a patient base of 43,000. The power of DaVita's repeatable formula is reflected in what happened at Gambro. The company's operating profit margin, at acquisition, was 8.9 percent, while DaVita's was 17.5 percent. Today, the Gambro centers are fully integrated into the network, achieving levels of financial and patient performance similar to DaVita's. The financial bottom line for this renewal around a repeatable model? From March 2000 through June 2011 DaVita was the best performing stock in the S&P 500, making a twenty-nine-fold return for investors who held the stock over this time.

The DaVita story holds a number of key lessons:

- Businesses can create a powerful, repeatable model later in their life if they have some strong, differentiated assets to build on (in DaVita's case it was the network of center locations and the base of patients).

- The importance of strongly driving the metrics, the vision, and the core values (and nonnegotiables) cannot be overestimated. It is what shortens the distance between the C-suite and the front line.

- A well-developed, repeatable formula can add considerable value in acquisitions, and enable combinations that would not have made sense before.

Some Ideas to Get You Started

We have tried in this discussion of the growing power of principles in strategy to include examples of businesses, like MSC and DaVita and LEGO, that have discovered that these ideas could help to revive and refocus a business, resulting in a real resurgence of profitable growth. Similarly, we have included examples like NIKE, which has experienced a couple of periods of stall-out, but has used the power of principles to renew its core business model and its growth trajectory. These ideas are not only for businesses that seem to have been born with these ideas—perhaps like Vanguard and IKEA.

There is no shortage of ways that the management team of a business might begin to use some of these ideas. We would especially suggest thinking about three of them.

First, try to understand the extent to which your management team agrees on the core principles of the strategy, the underlying value drivers in the industry, and your beliefs system. Then ask how the most important and practical dimensions of the strategy have been translated into a set of nonnegotiable behaviors. Perhaps you already have these and they are working perfectly—that would be the rare exception. Then the hard part: determine whether these are recognized and understood at different levels down to the front line. What really is the gap across the management team and from the management team down into the key functions of the company? If these gaps are large, it is probably worth taking the time to drive a process through discussion sessions and workshops to close them. The more consistent the agreement and understanding of the nonnegotiables of the business, the faster and more responsive your company will be.

Second, once you have identified the most important nonnegotiables that you really want to drive focus and behavior, take just one and follow it down to see how it is translated into actions and routines that drive behavior. Ask yourself whether this varies enormously across the organization and whether the key data is transparent—as in the examples above of Enterprise (NPS) or AB InBev (cost measures). This simple undertaking may give you some good insight on barriers to learning and to more effective performance. The more consistent and transparent the nonnegotiables are, the greater the ability to learn, to identify and share best practices, and to interpret performance.

Finally, ask yourself and your team these questions about the business that you are closest to or most concerned with:

- Can the strategy be stated in a small number of principles?

- Does the senior team agree with them? Are they shared broadly?

- Are they translated into operating nonnegotiables and routines that drive frontline execution and aid in making difficult decisions?

- What is the distance from the management team to the front line?

- Are you happy with the speed and consistency of the organization?

- What are the three most important nonfinancial measures of the health of your business model? Do you all agree?

We turn next to the third design principle of the Great Repeatable Models: the importance of a system of closed-loop feedback to the front line, the customers, and beyond.

Principle 3: Closed-Loop Learning

The Dutch flower auction in Aalsmeer, The Netherlands, takes place in one of the largest enclosed commercial buildings in the world—larger than 120 soccer fields. At precisely 6 a.m. every day, hundreds of buyers assemble in the five auction rooms of FloraHolland in Aalsmeer to buy fresh cut flowers and plants. Anxious bidders sit with fingers on buttons as an electronic clock signals the remaining time and the current price in one auction after another—each usually lasting no more than a few seconds. Below the clock is a kaleidoscopic procession of colored flowers in three-tier carts representing the lots.

In just a few hours, FloraHolland trades 45 million cut flowers and 5 million plants in some 120,000 transactions involving more than 7,500 growers. FloraHolland has captured a 40 percent market share of cut flowers in Europe, a 65 percent share of cut tulips, 95 percent of wholesale flowers sold by auction in Europe, and an amazing 98 percent of the Dutch market. If you laid end-to-end the cut flowers sold in a day at Aalsmeer, the line would stretch from Holland to the Himalayas. Thanks to FloraHolland's remarkable success, fees from its flower auction business have grown from 23 million euros in 1975 to nearly 380 million euros today. It has now almost completely consolidated the flower auctions business, driving enormous efficiency and a scale that makes it the only business that can assemble a complete set of flower offerings in one place.

After their purchase, the flowers are dispatched in one of FloraHolland's 270,000 auction trolleys to adorn dinner tables and renew romances around the world. The perishable nature of flowers (they lose more than 10 percent of their value every day), the increasingly long supply chains, and the instant nature of information technology place a premium on speed and consistency, both of which characterize the operations at FloraHolland.

Indeed, spending a day there is like watching a well-choreographed ballet. Every action—from the flower handlers who display the product to the bidders, to the operators who re-sort the carts of flowers by shipment destination—is tightly linked and directed toward a single purpose: to ensure that each flower arrives at the end of its long journey successfully. You can observe all this from a glass-enclosed platform that snakes its way from the flower-filled stage under the auction clocks to the re-sorting room, to the robotically controlled carts that shuttle off on computer-controlled tracks to trucks and planes nearby. The routine is now so efficient that a rose picked in Kenya on Wednesday can be auctioned in Holland on Thursday morning and be on a restaurant table in Stockholm the same night.

Like many Great Repeatable Models, FloraHolland has been around a long time. Flower auctions in Holland trace back to the early 1600s and the tulip mania. With the improvements of transportation in the early 1900s, growers began banding together as cooperatives to sell their flowers directly to buyers in Holland on a regional basis, using the Dutch auction method, where prices start high and decline until there is a buyer—the opposite of traditional auctions, but a very time-efficient method for reaching the selling price of a disposable item.

Over the past century, many innovations, such as digital clocks, the Internet, and new transportation systems, have threatened to change the business. Each time, FloraHolland has been the most successful adapter—a testament not only to the distinct simplicity of its strategy and the amazing coordination of its operations, but to the third feature of its Great Repeatable Model: its ability to continuously learn, improve, and adapt. It's thanks to this ability that FloraHolland has been able to escape the winner's curse.

Competition attacks pockets of success—profit pools and business models that create value—and the greatest success usually draws the strongest competition. In a slower world, fast adaptability used to be a "nice to have" in an organization. In the increasingly complicated organizations of today, facing a world in which reaction cycles are shrinking and competitive advantage is more fleeting, it is a must-have. Indeed, it's because of the importance of adaptability that people believe that reinvention is the source of competitive advantage. As we'll see, though, the adaptability of Great Repeatable Models is based on something very different.

In this chapter, we'll explain how superior learning processes confer an advantage, and we'll describe the learning systems of businesses that have put in place mechanisms to help them adapt faster. The essence and the power of this design principle of Great Repeatable Models is the ability to manage risks of adaptation better, not simply to encourage faster taking of more risks. Let's begin, however, by recognizing the extent of the challenge that adaptability presents.

The Elusiveness of Adaptability

In principle, a business built around a well-defined differentiation and an organization predicated on clear, well-internalized values should be able to perform much better than the average (more complex, less transparent) business on all four stages of the learning cycle: recognition, interpretation, decision, and mobilization. Recognition should be easier for an organization that shares from top to bottom a consistent vocabulary and can gather comparable information across the business versus the "pattern of no pattern." Interpretation, in the absence of hubris (a big and sometimes not easy requirement), should be easier given a common worldview, a set of core principles, and appropriate metrics on which to focus. Decision should be faster in a business that has simplified around a model with agreement on what really matters and the principles to drive some of the key trade-offs. Finally, mobilization should be more effective in an aligned organization with a shorter effective distance from the CEO to the front line.

It's not as simple as that, of course, especially in a period of sustained success, when the least risky path in the long term may be the most risky path in the short term (because reaction can be distracting and consume energy in the absence of a "burning platform" or crisis). The data shows that although adaptive systems were important for high performers, there was a less marked difference between the best and the worst performers—essentially because no one is fantastic at adaptability. In our two hundred–company database, well-defined processes to adapt (the four phases listed above) were felt to exist (a 4 or 5 rating on a scale of 1 to 5) in 48 percent of the best quintile of performers and in only 9 percent of the other four quintiles (see figure 4-1). But when we probed with questions on the relative superiority of the adaptive systems, we found agreement with the statement that the company had superior

FIGURE 4-1

Adherence to design principle 3: closed-loop learning

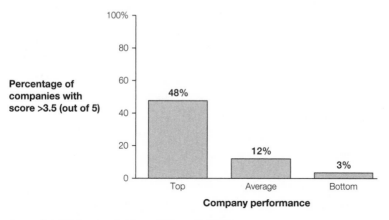

Source: Bain 200 Company Database of Repeatable Models.

learning systems in only 36 percent of the top quintile in performance, 10 percent for the average performers and 6 percent
for the bottom performers. When we constrained this further
to "strongly agree," the percentages all dropped markedly, from
18 percent for the top performers to 0 percent for the bottom
group. Clearly, learning is the least developed of the three Great
Repeatable Model design principles across all companies. It's a
new and increasingly important source of competitive advantage in many industries, waiting for superiority to emerge.

Our survey of 377 global executives in March 2011 also bore
this out.[1] More than two-thirds of executives said that the ability
to adapt is becoming a much more important factor in competitive advantage in their industry. More than half of respondents
said that the pace of change was making it much harder to adapt
and execute strategies in time, and that the company that they
viewed as their main competitor today would not be the same
one in only five years—all signs of a growing premium on the
systems and skills of adaptation.

Our case examples led to the same conclusion. Many well-documented studies by business historians reveal how successful business models can breed the seeds of their own rigidity, lack of learning, and eventual decline through complacency, hubris, a lack of willingness to question basic assumptions, and other human foibles. The travails of Kodak, Xerox, General Motors, AOL, Sony, U.S. Steel, Sainsbury's, LEGO (in the 1980s and '90s), Nokia, Dell, Microsoft (with regard to the role of the Internet), and Kmart can be seen in this light, as cases of "arrested adaptation"—fantastic formulas that did not change fast enough and ended up in catch-up mode. Most of these examples, we should note, were not cases of amazing and sudden "disruptive" innovations that caught the incumbent flat-footed. As we described earlier, both our studies and those of others suggest that cases of stall-out or stagnation are much more often the result of slow response over time to many signs along the way—an organization that was not good at learning—than failure to see and prepare for a huge disruption.

Of course, it's not always a company problem. Sometimes entire industries do go through a cycle of growth, maturity, and decline, to be replaced by businesses with completely different models. Horses shifted to automobiles. Typewriters shifted to word processors. Book retailing shifted to online information downloading. Long-distance train and boat travel was replaced by the airplane. Wired telephony switched to wireless. The list is long. However, much longer is the list of industries that shifted by 20 percent or 30 percent, leaving many of the core capabilities of the companies in them highly relevant. These are the cases where superior mechanisms to react faster, and to buy more time, would make an enormous difference in the survivability and life expectancy of businesses.

In fact, even for some of the more extreme "paradigm shifts," you could still argue that incumbents possessed most of the assets needed to adapt and survive. Take the case of Kodak, whose share price has collapsed to less than $4, from $80 in 1996, because it lost the battle for the digital customer. Yet, many of its key assets in photography were not under threat from the technology shift and offered robust platforms on which to build a leading digital business—access to customers, brand, lenses and optics, distribution channels, manufacturing of metal precision housings, and so on. Kodak even possessed some of the core digital technology. For instance, even today, the sensor in the highest-end form of camera—the Leica M9—is a Kodak digital sensor. The "transformation" was dramatic, but really only applied to about half of the value chain. The problem was not a lack of assets, resources, or even ability to see the digital shift—it was inability to mobilize and adapt the model fast enough. To compound matters, Kodak went through four CEO changes, each CEO with his own strategy and none really gaining traction, during the key decade of transition to digital. This is a tough way to adapt one of the Great Repeatable Models.

The decay rate of success in business underscores the challenge and rarity of successful adaptation. To look at this, we returned to our sustained value creator companies of earlier. Using more than twenty-five years of data, we looked at the major companies globally that for each ten-year period achieved this performance threshold (earning the cost of capital and growing revenues and profits by more than 5.5 percent in real terms). We found that on average less than one in five of these high performers in any given decade maintained their sustained performance over the next decade.

In this respect, business seems to closely reflect the natural world. Biologist Stuart Pimm has analyzed fossils to estimate the rate of extinction of plants, birds, mussels, and mammals. He found a one hundred to one thousand times increase in the rate of extinction since the dominance of the human race on earth, which he attributed to environmental shifts such as destruction of rain forests, intrusion into African wilderness, and contamination of the ocean. He predicts that the extinction rate will rise tenfold in the next century as a greater rate of environmental change outstrips the natural rate of evolution. Fortunately for business, the analogy doesn't stretch so far. Unlike animals and plants, businesses fail to adapt not because they can't but because they won't. Business failure is the consequence of decisions, not circumstances, and most wrong decisions are rooted in internal, avoidable cognitive and psychological dynamics.

The Challenges of Adaptability

Controllable human factors, in the presence of plenty of time to react, are at the center of most of the case studies we examined of failure to adapt or to change the fundamentals of a business model in response to external developments. This parallels the findings of Irving Janis in his classic book *Groupthink*.[2] Janis examined a series of well-documented government decisions that went wrong, such as the Bay of Pigs invasion of Cuba. He found that in each case, the leadership team screened out important information from the outside and discarded alternative points of view that were not consistent with what they wanted to believe. Time and again, the root cause of disaster was a self-induced lack of self-awareness.

The psychological inhibitors that created this state of mind were natural human reactions to dissonance or to change, taken to the extreme. One was pure denial, the refusal to accept that the historical success factors (elements of the past model) were becoming obsolete, and the disinclination to examine contrary data with an urgent mind. A second factor was ignorance due to distorted information from the outside and from the front line, the distortion dulling a sense of urgency. Many of the examples of technologies attacking an incumbent from the bottom of the market, such as those featured in Clayton Christensen's classic book on this subject, *The Innovator's Dilemma*, fall into this category.[3] Third was an energy deficit. Change and risk takes energy, and energy to address the real problems becomes scarce in times of short-term crisis (due to long-term factors). Energy is directed to defend the status quo rather than to question or change it. Decades of failing to reduce costs or consolidate the airline industry in the face of low-cost carriers is an example of this.

A fourth factor is fear itself. Threats to your core are scary, and launching major change programs is even scarier, especially since this is a one-off in the life of most executives, giving them a limited base of past experience to draw on. It is perhaps why many of the most dramatic cases of changes were by new CEOs brought in under conditions of crisis. Examples would include the turnarounds of LEGO, IBM, Marvel Entertainment, and DaVita, all of which needed new, aggressive CEOs to drive them. Finally, there is the pure risk and physical level of difficulty. It is always easier to hold on for one more quarter, driving quarterly earnings from the model of the past, than to confront massive change and deal with it. And, sometimes, the needed change is not obvious. The travails of the major newspapers around the world in the face of the Internet and digital media are a case in point.

There can be no simple panacea for businesses with a model that needs to adapt and a management team feeling anxiety, fatigue, resource scarcity, the pressure of quarterly earnings, and uncertainty about what the right answer may be. However, one thing can be said with relative certainty: it is better to see the problem sooner—and this is possible with clearer and more transparent data.

Let's switch gears now to look at the enablers rather than the barriers to adaptability.

Learning: Apple's Hidden Story

Research on top performers in fields from music to sports shows that the most successful individuals practice more methodically than lower performers and have more structured feedback systems built into their practice routines. The higher performers have also been found, on average, to react differently—more open-mindedly and with greater concern—than lower performers to new information about their technique. Geoff Colvin in his book *Talent Is Overrated* (perhaps somewhat analogous to our theme in this book where we observe the same thing applied to businesses) finds:

> Top performers in a wide range of fields have better organized and consolidated their knowledge, enabling them to approach problems in fundamentally different and more useful ways. For example, accomplished physicists and beginning physics students were given two dozen physical problems and asked to sort them by type of problem. The beginners sorted the problems according to their most obvious features, such as whether they involved friction or an inclined plane. The more expert physicists sorted them by the basic principles—say, Newton's second law—that would be needed to solve them . . . In general, the knowledge of top performers is integrated and connected to higher level principles.[4]

To bring this to life in a business context, let's look at the case of Apple. There can be few more remarkable and more closely followed stories of corporate renewal than this one. Apple was founded on April Fools' Day in 1976, with the mission to create an easier-to-use personal computer. But despite succeeding at this mission in the eyes of most industry observers, Apple's overall success was mixed. In 1996 the company had less than 5 percent global market share in personal computers, was stalled in the marketplace, and posted operating losses of $1.4 billion on revenues of $9.8 billion. Today, Apple's 2010 revenues exceeded $65 billion, with pretax profit of more than $18 billion. Except for a short six-month stock price burst in the Internet bubble period, Apple's stock price for more than twenty years (1980–2002) bounced between $1 and $10 per share; today it is more than $300 per share.[5] Founder Steve Jobs left Apple at its lowest point in 1985, returning to engineer its resurgence in September 1997.

Apple since inception had at its core an operating system with superior ease of use, the best in multimedia, and superior design. But despite these differentiating factors, the personal computer market was not where these capabilities were able to reach their full potential. Most users of computers were in business, where the lower-cost offerings of Dell, IBM, and HP, fueled by Windows software and Intel chips, proved to be a more economical solution in terms of total cost of ownership. Through it all, however, Apple clung on, leveraging its core and its young and "technology forward" base of promoters. As the markets for computing technology and software evolved, this value proposition came into its own; since Jobs's return, Apple has exploited and replicated it very effectively.

It is hard to believe that the first iPod was launched as recently as November 2001, given its impact on the world. Since then, major new launches have included multiple generations of iPod, iTunes, iPhone, and iPad. Yet, there's a consistent discipline in the way Apple manages this stream of innovation. In its iPod launches, for example, Apple carefully limits the number of device types and models (classic, shuffle, nano, and touch), and it retires models as it reduces the features (for instance, the iPod classic used to come in four storage sizes; today it comes only in 160 GB).

This is clearly a company with a strong, enduring, differentiated core, with a repeatable model since the return of Steve Jobs that exploits it into new segments and applications, and with strong internal values—the archetype of our focus in this book. That much is well known. But when you look more closely at the Apple business model, you soon realize that Apple also possesses the third feature of the Great Repeatable Model, and that this characteristic has enabled it to maintain and keep replicating its differentiations so effectively. In fact, few companies, with the possible exception of Google, have as many methods to capture and use customer feedback. For instance:

- *The Genius Bar.* Before the advent of the direct retail channel, Apple had relatively few direct customer contacts; most were through channels. But how that has changed today. Now, the technical service people at the Genius Bar, where customers are assisted with their computer problems and questions, collect and sort their notes to find repeatable issues on products. All the data is aggregated, sorted by product, and channeled to the right place in the company. There is a culture now at retail that is linked to Apple's overall culture of innovating and taking risks. Apple uses many forms of feedback at the store level to refine experiments and see how people react to the company's constant adaptations and changes.

- *Store Net Promoter score (NPS).* When you make a purchase at an Apple store, you will receive an electronic receipt and sometimes a short survey of two questions regarding your visit and whether you would recommend the store. Any negative responses are followed up on by store managers, and the overall results are shared at the store and then aggregated and passed up the chain. This is especially critical for new launches, where Apple can compare the scores at a launch and probe systematically for reactions and issues.

- *Store-level data collection.* Apple is able to use its iPod touch in the store to do efficient exit surveys of buyers and nonbuyers to try to understand in more detail what happens with customers who had an intention to buy but left without doing so. One illustrative discovery was that the stores were so crowded that customers had trouble identifying salespeople in their black T-shirts—Apple changed to brighter, characteristic colors and found that reduced the problem.

- *Online data collection.* The company's Web sites— notably the App Store, the online Apple Store, and iTunes—also provide a great deal of information on general buying patterns.

The power of these and many other sources of feedback that Apple gathers on its products and customers is made all the more powerful by Apple's discipline in maintaining simplicity in products and simplicity in its business model. It is possible for Steve Jobs to review all corporate product initiatives at a single Monday meeting. As he says, "Every Monday we review the whole business. We look at every single product under development. I put out an agenda. Eighty percent of it is the same as it was the last week, and we just walk down it every single week."[6] The result is what one person at Apple has referred to as "constant course correction."

Our discussions with people at Apple on this topic reveal a constant recognition of the power of simplification in the ability of Apple to adapt. One spoke about the fact that the major product tests and experiments are hardwired all the way to the top of the company, enormously reducing the distance from the CEO to the front line. Another described how Apple has only about fifty core product codes made at its outsourcer Foxconn, whereas some companies in the consumer electronics and computer businesses have more than fifteen thousand.

Apple is not the only company to discover the power of robust learning systems. LEGO Group, which we discussed in chapter 2, has put in place similar learning systems to make sure that its model stays relevant to customers:

- *Net Promoter scores* are now collected at each customer touch point (shops, online, consumer services, etc.) and for each major product category. These are distributed throughout the company on a monthly basis, and all negative responses are followed up on individually. The data is now moving to an online real-time platform to drive even faster action and to capture learning, and the scores have improved 26 percent since 2005.

- *The Kids Inner Circle* was started as an online community of five thousand children, by invitation only, who love to interact with LEGO in this way on new products in process.

- *A "quick poll" system* has been put in place to receive reactions on specific themes, features, and stories as LEGO Group works on new products.

- *One hundred thirty-five company-sponsored LEGO shows* have drawn 2.6 million visitors, from which user groups totaling 65,000 members have been created. More than eighty cocreation projects were done with these groups in 2009 alone.

It's compelling logic. Let's look now in more detail at what it is about the systems at Apple, LEGO Group, and other Great Repeatable Models that makes them so effective.

Introducing the OODA Loop

We believe that the best framework for thinking about the relative competitive power of systems for learning and decision making remains the OODA loop, which was first codified in a military context by the legendary and iconoclastic U.S. fighter pilot John Boyd.

During the Korean War, Boyd began to develop his ideas about competition between adversaries' different decision cycles. He was trying to explain why American aviators had a ten-to-one success rate against their opponents even though the American plane, the F-86, was thought to be inferior on most performance measures to its opponent, the MiG-15. He concluded that the F-86 had two small advantages that proved to make an enormous difference. First, it had better visibility to the outside; and second, the nature of its hydraulic controls meant that it could change tactics faster. As a result, the American pilots were able to *observe* external change better, *orient* themselves to their situation more clearly, *decide* what to do with higher certainty, and *act* slightly faster—and the OODA loop (a letter for each step) was born (see figure 4-2). Boyd spent much of the rest of his life expanding this concept into a legendary fourteen-hour presentation on the OODA loop, never put into a book (but you can find the original presentation still on the Internet), and using his insights to inform next-generation plane design and pilot training.[7]

Boyd's insight, which is increasingly applicable in fast-moving business markets, was that if you can operate within

FIGURE 4-2

John Boyd's OODA loop

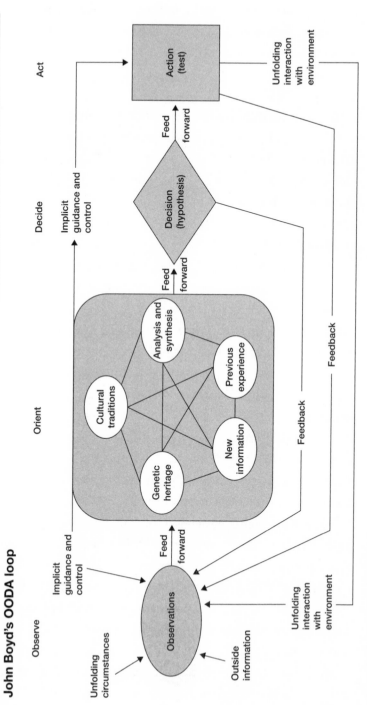

Source: John Boyd presentation materials.

your competitor's decision loop, you have an enormous tactical advantage on the battlefield. Furthermore, he and his working group felt that while all four phases of the decision loop were critical, it was the orientation phase that was the most differentiating in competitive conditions—how to take raw information streaming in from the outside, quickly interpret it, discard extraneous noise, and direct it toward the right decision quickly. As the work on OODA loops has proceeded, it has become increasingly rich, for, in reality, there are many different OODA loops in most competitive situations. Furthermore, decision loops have both offensive implications and disruptive implications about slowing or confusing the decision processes of an adversary. In the case of the MiGs against the F-86s in Korea, often the MiG pilots would see the advantage unfolding in the air and panic because there was nothing they could do about it. It was almost as if they no longer controlled their own decision process—as indeed they did not. One student of Boyd writes of this phenomenon, "By the time their opponent acted, they were doing something different. With each cycle, the slower side's actions were less apt and it fell farther and farther behind. This is what happened in many of history's most decisive battles. Hannibal went through the OODA loop faster than the Romans at Cannae and won one of history's greatest tactical victories."[8]

We discussed earlier the advantages of a superior repeatable model in business in terms of greater speed to decide and act, and superior focus and alignment at the front line. A faster and better decision loop is one of the most important mainsprings of this impact. If you talk to competitors of companies that made rapid market share advances with a faster-moving and superior strategy, the competitors feel as if they have lost control over their own strategy. Examples would be the triumph of Dell in the mid-1990s against traditional PC sellers, the relentless and repeatable onslaught of Apple from the iPod through the iPad, the acquisition machines that GE Capital and Vodafone built to preempt competitors by their speed of buying and integrating companies, or the suddenness by which Mittal Steel (now known as ArcelorMittal) acted to consolidate and become the world's largest steel company. In each case, you see the multiplier effect of a superior repeatable formula in combination with a more rapid decision cycle than had been typical in the industry.

At the time he was doing his work for the military, John Boyd felt that the Toyota system was the best example he had seen of the power of a fast OODA loop in the context of business to drive constant learning and fast adjustment—the heart of continuous improvement, which we have emphasized over and over as an area where the Great Repeatable Model companies can drive powerful advantage.

Superior speed and quality of decision making is a competitive weapon that is becoming of increasing importance in a world of increasing speed and complexity. Marcia Blenko, Michael Mankins, and Paul Rogers recently completed a study of organizational effectiveness (reported in their book *Decide and Deliver*).[9] They studied 760 companies worldwide through 39 questions regarding perceptions of decision speed, quality, and ability to execute. The responses came from many levels of the organization. When the authors synthesized these responses into an index of decision effectiveness, they found that top-quintile companies on decisions produced an average total shareholder return about 6 percentage points higher than that of other companies. Companies with strong feedback loops driving a well-defined repeatable business model should have the potential to be superior on all three of these elements.

The Sources of Learning

Feedback can flow in many ways in an organization, and it's not our intention to catalog all of them or identify the most important. It really depends on your specific business. That being said, it is worth highlighting the more common feedback loops that we found repeated in the Great Repeatable Models we studied. The primary distinction we use to categorize them is the source of information.

Learning from the Core Customer

The most common feedback loop in Great Repeatable Models is direct, immediate customer feedback. The simplest and most powerful way we have seen this done is through the use of NPS systems, used at LEGO and Apple as described earlier. This approach is usually based on asking one or two questions of the customer shortly after contact about their satisfaction with that contact and their willingness to recommend. The great power of the NPS approach lies in its simplicity. Companies that chase more detailed feedback typically find that customers don't bother to engage, and they get less and poorer data as a result. By limiting the questions, however, you get higher response rates and better information—leading to better-grounded decisions in the first place. Customers are also more likely to participate in the survey multiple times, allowing a rapid cycling of test-response loops in product/service experiments. The founder of Charles Schwab credits NPS as a major contributor to turning around the company. In the year after it was put in place, Schwab's revenues increased by 11 percent, customer scores by 25 percent, new brokerage accounts by 10 percent, and net assets increased despite the financial crisis.

In more complex environments, companies with direct sales forces have interesting opportunities to create powerful OODA feedback loops with customers. Take the case of the toolmaker Hilti. Founded in 1941 by Martin Hilti as a mechanical workshop with five employees in Schaan, Liechtenstein, the company was focused on innovative tools for difficult construction jobs from the start, with the creation of a device to pound nails pneumatically. The product worked well, but the first versions were dangerous and needed a further round of innovation on piston mechanics to maintain force while reducing speed, so that the nails did not shoot out like bullets. Martin Hilti's people spent much time at the job site, observing and interacting with customers. This would ground his design choices that he would then rapidly prototype with the customers to learn about their limitations. This was the start of the Hilti direct sales force, which remains a core part of the Hilti model today. Over the following decades, the business grew one tool at a time; the company would obtain the basic design and then innovate intensively on the details that would make it more perfect for specific customer applications at the job site.

The evolution of the early repeatable formula led the company into a range of tools and systems for fastening, drilling, coring, anchoring, cutting, and hanging in heavy construction applications. The model also evolved its direct-to-customer sales and distribution by adding local sales and service branches and by being the first in the industry with telephone sales and service. Today, in an industry where about 75 percent of products are sold through indirect channels, this direct customer contact remains a differentiated strength. It is one of the reasons why Hilti is able to create innovations in the tools that capture significant price premiums over competitors. Commenting on this, its chairman and former CEO, Pius Baschera, said:

> We have one distinct advantage over most competitors—direct distribution. Let's complete a very simple calculation: if each one of our twelve thousand field employees visits ten to fifteen customers a day, between them they make well over one hundred fifty thousand customer contacts. That's every day. This is why we know exactly what our customers want. Our research and development doesn't "invent" products in a vacuum, in the hope that these appeal to the market. As a rule, they translate the customer's actual wishes—a hard enough task in itself. Incidentally, this applies not only to products, but also to services, in particular.[10]

The technology revolution has, of course, increased the range of customer feedback loops you can create. Amazon, another Great Repeatable Model, has one of the richest imaginable databases on customer browsing, buying, and response behaviors. This data and quick customer feedback online is used to tailor messages and notices at the level of the individual customer and, most important, to quickly test new service offerings in ways that no competitor can currently match.

In particular, companies that have traditionally marketed through third parties have found that new technologies make it easier for them to communicate directly with customers that used to be inaccessible. Swedish truck manufacturer Scania, for example, has decided that feedback from truck drivers through dealers is too slow and imperfect for the increasing level of closed-loop learning it is trying to drive, and now has put in place methods to talk directly to truck drivers on a continuous basis, with a pledge to address easy-to-fix problems in ten days and a full capture of feedback for longer-term modification.[11] The adoption of this direct loop has played a role in helping Scania transition from introducing product changes in batches through introducing new models to a continuous improvement system in which it makes new versions of the same models.

Other companies have gone even further in involving customer feedback in innovation. The Internet's capability in creating many-to-many communities has given rise to *crowd sourcing*—a method whereby consumers can offer design suggestions for products or (as with the open-source software of Wikipedia) help to solve problems collectively. Crowd sourcing is being used by an increasing number of companies, including Keds, Bloomingdale's, NIKE, and Coach, to involve large numbers of consumers in product design. It is also being used by Facebook to tailor the network software to local language and cultural conditions. One extreme example is at IBM, which has created a series of seventy-two-hour sessions it calls "InnovationJam." These sessions are organized around topics like innovation in health care, airports, or education. They are moderated online and are open to IBM employees and to others. IBM hopes that it can harness the power of as many as ninety thousand minds around a topic.

Learning from Key Operations

A second important set of feedback loops are systems that monitor and highlight key operating parameters, enabling managers both to react to problems and to share learning across the system. Small variations in the effectiveness of these systems at identifying, comparing, and reacting to variations in operating variables can add up to a large difference in competitive advantage over time, in terms of both cost control and product development.

The idea of the *experience curve*, defining the relatively predictable logarithmic relationship between repeated experiences in production and unit cost for a business or a manufacturing plant, has a long history. The relationship between accumulated units produced and cost was first studied by Nobel Prize–winning economist Kenneth Arrow.[12] It was developed as a central tool of business strategy by Bruce Henderson and applied especially to cost-based manufacturing businesses.[13] Walter Kiechel, in his extensive history of strategic thought in business, felt it was one of the seminal ideas of the last century: "The experience curve was, simply, the single most important concept in launching the strategy revolution . . . What the experience curve concept did was to instigate a sea change in the way that companies think about their costs."[14]

A continuing theme in this book is the power of achieving superiority in the speed of incremental improvement relative to your competitors, and the size of that compounding effect over time. A powerful example of this can be seen in the most iconic product of our first case study, IKEA. Figure 4-3 shows the experience curve of the Billy bookcase (measured by price to the consumer in inflation-adjusted terms). Despite the simplicity of this self-assembled bookcase, IKEA has continued to innovate on materials, fasteners, and construction details to drive the cost down by an astonishing 76 percent (in constant currency) from the price at its introduction in 1979!

Such learning curve trajectories can also be used to create a system across different units to visualize not only their relative costs, but also their relative rate of learning and improvement over time. A simple example of this is provided by the

FIGURE 4-3

Experience curve of the IKEA Billy bookcase

Real price of Billy bookcase (in 2009 constant USD)

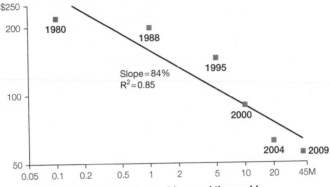

Number of Billy bookcases sold around the world

Note: Logarithmic scale used on both horizontal and vertical axes. Average of prices in various countries in Europe and North America.
Sources: Company Web site, literature search, Euromonitor, EIU.

global corporation whose factory unit cost curves are shown in figure 4-4. This company, a client, was operating close to sixty factories globally and was frustrated by its growing manufacturing costs. Hundreds of improvement projects had been regularly launched with detailed, thoughtful implementation plans. But no result was visible in the P&L—and the lack of progress was starting to hamper our client's ability to invest behind people and brands. When we gathered detailed perspectives from the supply chain executives across the system as well as from frontline employees in the factories, it became clear that there was no consistency, there were no common standards, and there was no repeatability or learning, despite the fact that manufacturing was viewed as an essential form of differentiation, and the company historically was strong in this area. Yet, inattention and complexity had set in. Typical factory tours or

FIGURE 4-4

Unit cost curves for European manufacturer

Production efficiency (unit costs)

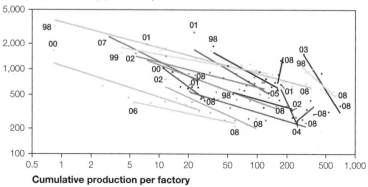

Cumulative production per factory

Source: Company data.

yearly performance reviews were nerve-racking for all parties. Senior executives were bombarded with hundreds of measurements, covering all levels of details (from the whole factory to the single production line), without a real focus on where the value was. Discussions always ended up in a mix of high-level patronizing guidelines and tense negotiations over targets. Every visit was different, and every discussion covered different themes. The one hundred manufacturing lines led to one hundred conversations.

Change started when the manufacturing community aligned on two simple principles that formed the basis of a new system for closed-loop learning and benchmarking, as well as a route back to repeatability in manufacturing operations. The first was that individual production lines were the relevant unit of repeatability, and the second one was that costs needed to decrease with experience at the best rate in the industry. The power of continuous improvement needed to be harnessed as a competitive weapon.

The company developed experience curves for the one hundred eighty manufacturing lines across the sixty factories globally. Since those lines were covering five different technologies, the company started to compare curves by technologies and was quickly able to define targets by line by factory, and not only for the next budgeting cycle, but for the long term. The first benefit of this simple, aligned approach was the clarity of dialogue between senior executives and the ability to set real targets versus relevant comparisons, as well as to learn and share practices across the system. In just the first few years, even this relatively basic system has completely changed the trajectory of the learning curves, and is driving savings of several hundred million euros, or about 3 percent of cost.

The engine that drives the experience curve is repeatable learning and improvement. We have found this to be relevant for the cost of widgets in a factory as well as for the efficiency of much more complex, integrated processes at the level of the whole business. We looked at this for two examples of Great Repeatable Models on the revenue side, versus the cost side, of the business. We found that key performance indicators—like the speed and success rate of entering new, adjacent markets with a proven formula—also improve along an experience curve.

The master at operational learning, of course, is Toyota, but enough has been written about that company that we need say no more here. Typically, though, operational learning systems are an important aspect of Great Repeatable Models whose key differentiations are not customer facing, such as Danaher's and AB InBev's, described in chapter 2. A common feature of these systems is that they are uniform across the organization and are designed for the information and solutions to be shared. Look at the description (on its Web site) by Scania of its Scania Production System (SPS), which it defines in terms of cocreation with employees, continuous improvement, and the ability to quickly disseminate best practices due to the uniformity it has achieved through its repeatable model: "SPS has been developed in-house by the company's own employees. SPS includes principles and methods that lead to continuously ongoing improvement work. Common working methods are applied at all Scania production units around the world . . . improvements introduced at one unit are disseminated systematically to other units in the global production network."[15]

On the one hand, you might look at this and say—of course. But on the other hand, we find that most businesses do not have well-developed comparative global systems driving continuous improvement at a world-class level. This is "low-hanging fruit" for businesses with dispersed manufacturing operations.

Learning from Frontline Employees

Frontline employees are the best source of information any company can have, if it is managed correctly. Most companies do annual surveys, but few are deeply scientific about the many ways of receiving feedback from the front line. This is one more reason why our concept of the distance from the CEO to the front line is front and center of this book.

This is the one case where we would like to offer an example of practices from our own company, Bain & Company. We have invested a great deal of effort in employee survey methods and believe that the use of this data is one reason Bain has been voted the best consulting firm in which to work (by employees) for the past nine years in a row.[16] Since its founding in 1973, Bain has achieved results that put it into the sustained value creator (SVC) category for every ten-year period, making it one of those relatively rare SVC companies that we examined. We believe that we live every day the three design principles of the

Great Repeatable Models. We have many systems for internal feedback and response.

Two are especially worth noting. First, we do an annual and quite extensive employee survey that we analyze by office, practice, level in the firm, and geography, and we share the results firmwide. We believe that this is one reason why employees rate Bain's culture 3.9 on a scale of 1 to 4 on the question of whether a unique culture is a positive differentiator for the firm. The second practice occurs after every project or phase of a major project. We do a *case team survey*, which is also shared with the project team and is a critical input into the performance of the managers. But the questions go far beyond "are you happy" questions and ask whether there was "yield loss" in the project and whether they felt that the project added enough value to the client, and why. This is incredibly valuable data for us to have across projects as we try to understand and replicate success factors.

Managers of businesses should take a quick inventory of their feedback and learning systems all the time. Relative to their expectations. Relative to the best companies. Relative to competitors. For employees, for core customers, for key operating points, and, perhaps, for competitors. There should be a clear sense of the most important data and a method to ensure its objectivity, its transparency, and its connection to action. This is, and will increasingly become, an important source of differentiation among companies. Just think of the compounding mathematics over five years of even relatively small trends in "continuous improvement" across all of these dimensions (imagine the long-term effects, for example, of the number of contacts with customers made by Hilti's sales force compared to contacts made by competitors). It is this arithmetic that fuels economies of scale and the total experience curve for a company over time—for if one competitor learns from multiple episodes at a faster rate than another, that competitor will achieve greater advantages of scale at a point in time and from its accumulated experience over time.

Managing the Learning Loops

Feedback-response loops need to be thought through in some detail, especially in complex businesses. This is a particular issue for companies with multiple layers of distribution and, therefore, multiple levels of customers responding. Moreover, there is often a different frequency of reporting, ranging from immediate for frontline follow-up on negative customer responses to quarterly reports across topics, businesses, or products. A good example of how to deal with this challenge can be seen in the structure of the recently implemented system. Moreover, as we saw with the discussion of the Danaher and UTC repeatable formulas, complex businesses like these can benefit enormously from a repeatable management system to manage across disparate situations with some consistency. It also acts as a lever that enables talent movement across disparate business situations, given the common language, operating discipline, systems, and processes are used consistently. Danaher has cited publicly that its rapid growth is made possible by having sufficient internal talent experienced with its Danaher Business System (DBS) capable of dropping into acquired businesses or being challenged with the biggest organic growth opportunities.

Figure 4-5 shows a simple schematic of the different feedback loops employed in the case of one large company that recently made a major investment in putting in place a system for more comprehensive customer feedback, based primarily on Net Promoter scores (the percentage difference between customers who are promoters, rating you as a 9 or 10, and those who are not

FIGURE 4-5

Typical system for closed-loop feedback at all levels

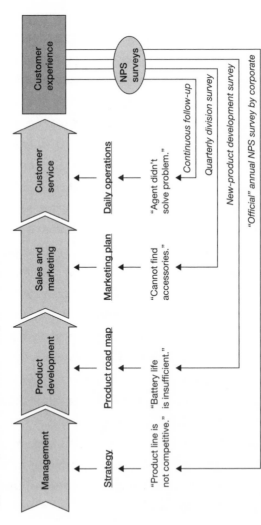

Source: Company materials.

promoters, rating you from 0 to 6). You can see on the right a rapid loop directly to people at the front line who are empowered to contact the customer and take immediate action. There is a second loop, where results are collected by product, customer type, and geography and fed into marketing; a third loop for product development based on the feedback; and a fourth, higher loop that links more broadly to strategy and the overall plan for that particular business. Finally it can all be examined, compared, and aggregated at the corporate level.

In managing the learning loops, you should bear in mind that adaptation and learning take place in terms of three time frames, each of which has its own OODA loop, its own system, and its own way of turning superiority into a real competitive advantage. The first is the short-term market feedback from frontline observation, customer feedback, plant-level tracking systems, or Net Promoter scores, for instance. These feedback systems and how frontline employees are empowered to decide and react on their own can be the difference between competitive advantage and disadvantage. Just think of the waitstaff at your local restaurants—some avoid your eyes and keep you waiting, and others seem almost intuitively to sense what you need. You notice that. The second rhythm of feedback systems is medium term—say, the time of a product adaptation. This is an area that some companies, like Apple or Procter & Gamble, epitomize. Huawei, the Chinese network equipment company is commonly viewed in the marketplace as faster to the ball in bids and installation. The company even has an Office of Constant Change that reports to the CEO. This is what we mean by medium-term feedback loops and speed.

The learning systems we have described so far fall into the short- and medium-term time frames. But obviously, companies also need to have systems to uncover, process, and adapt to changes whose impact is longer term and sometimes more threatening to the business model itself, rare as that might be.

We turn now to these somewhat different processes, whereby fundamental threats to the business models of the past, or the rules of the game in an industry, are confronted.

Strategic Learning

Although the turnaround of IBM is well documented, the magnitude of the numbers never fails to impress. The 1980s were a great decade for IBM, during which it attained 40 percent market share and 70 percent profit pool share of computers. Yet, by 1992 IBM's stock price had collapsed with the advent of the PC and the new, superior business models of companies like Dell. IBM in desperation had already shed sixty thousand jobs and thereafter replaced its CEO with Lou Gerstner. At the time, IBM stood for "big iron," and services were only 27 percent of the company. In his memoir, Gerstner says, "The company didn't lack for smart, talented people. Its problems weren't fundamentally technical in nature. It had file drawers full of winning strategies. Yet the company was frozen in place."[17]

The barriers, in Gerstner's mind, were the company's inability to adapt to new models, the profit pool shift to software, and many other smaller factors everywhere you looked. As another commentator noted, the challenge of IBM had become "to learn better how to serve the customer, integrate the organization around the customer's needs, and to transform themselves from a great product company to one that solved customers' problems."[18] Today, IBM has put in place a range of changes to improve on the four dimensions of capturing better external feedback, interpreting it, driving decisions, and pushing to actions.

The new process consists of two pieces relating to fundamental decisions around the business model or product offerings—one called the strategic insight process and the other the strategic execution process. Major issues that come up from the company's windows on the marketplace and customers are driven through both processes in a relatively repeatable way. The study cited above indicated that from 1999 to 2005, eighteen such issues were identified, from how to deal with Linux to digital media to the emergence of blade servers.[19] The decision process has been made more continuous (versus a yearly cycle), much more open regarding the issues of concern, and much more involving of people with many different perspectives. Moreover, there are different cycles depending on the issue, from monthly technology team cycles to longer cycles for the large strategic issues and shorter cycles at the front line. Since the core of the turnaround, from 1996 to 2005, IBM increased its share price relative to the S&P 500 index by 82 percent—perhaps in part due to processes that speed and highlight areas where adaptation is essential.

One of the best institutional processes for strategic learning, particularly powerful in dynamic, fast-changing industries, was put in place by Sir Christopher Gent, CEO of Vodafone. Coincidentally, Gent began his career with the company on the same day as its shares started trading, and the learning process Vodafone established coincided with the turbulent period when wireless telephone networks were undergoing rapid global expansion. During this period, Vodafone grew from a small regional carrier in the United Kingdom in 1988 to global leader in 2003 with revenues of almost $50 billion, more than three times the size of its next largest competitor. Vodafone faced five major forks in the road, each of which would shape the future course and adaptation of the evolving global Vodafone model. For example, the company needed to decide whether to continue to invest in land-based systems (it chose to focus on its wireless core) or what to do with its small infrastructure manufacturing business (it decided to outsource the making of equipment).

The strategic learning process Gent put in place was called Brocket Hall because it took place in that off-site location. Gent convened Vodafone's senior managers for a week to review the major strategic choices facing the business, rigorously rate major growth opportunities, and debate a set of predetermined questions such as these:

- Does this strengthen and reinforce our core model?

- What is our future differentiation and how does each opportunity add?

- Can this create a repeatable model for rollout across the world?

- Does each opportunity add to critical capabilities for the future?

- Do we have the capacity to implement and will it distract from our core business?

- How do the opportunities and threats relate to each other? How do we rank them?

A high-profile process with a regular rhythm and structured methods to ensure objective outside input is essential for any company that depends on success in turbulent markets for its survival. Yet, our data shows, most businesses are not excellent here. More low-hanging fruit to pluck.

The idea of investing in systems to adapt much more self-consciously as a source of competitive advantage is much more than a "cut and paste" to repeatable models; it is much more fundamental. In fact, you can view each of the three design principles of the Great Repeatable Models as setting a company up for focused innovation and for making speed of response a competitive advantage. In fact, the three design principles are all essentially "outside-in" in their nature. The idea that strategy starts with deep capabilities and differentiation relative to competition is an externally focused view of business. The second design principle is directed at reducing the distance from the CEO to the front line and to the marketplace—also externally focused. And we have talked about the elements of the third design principle—well-developed systems to acquire, process, and use market feedback. In a sense, we are reducing strategy to its elements—deep and unique capabilities, understood by the whole organization, and a "best in class" method to tailor and adapt them to a changing world. This is becoming the essence of strategy, and systems for learning are becoming a new "essential test" of the robustness of all strategies.

Ideas into Action

In one sense, the idea that methods to monitor and adjust the key elements of the strategy of a business sounds so obvious as to be unnecessary to even state. Yet, our collective fifty years of doing strategy consulting has proved to us the opposite. It is the rare business that insists that every newly developed strategy includes explicit methods to monitor, test, evaluate, respond, and adapt. In a world of constant change, our conclusions point to the reality that what was once an optional feature is now a requirement of robust strategy. Every strategy that is accepted by a management team should be accompanied by some discussion of its key OODA loops.

It is impossible to be precisely prescriptive about the best set of processes in order to increase the odds of adapting to change faster and better than your competitors. It depends on the dynamics of your industry, the practices of your competitors, the speed of technology evolution, the capital intensity and irreversibility of key decisions, and the nature of the customers. However, there are a few ideas that all organizations might think about to get started.

First, consider taking a hard look at your most important methods for learning and adaptation of your core business model against short-, medium-, and longer-term change. Do an inventory and an assessment. What has been their track record? Are you forcing your competitors to react to you, outside of your decision cycle? Is your responsiveness a competitive advantage or not? Should it be? How would you know? Is the learning that drives constant improvement (think of the Billy bookcase) a competitive advantage? Are you taking advantage of the power of constant learning?

Second, return to the idea of the distance from the management team to the front line and the customer. Look over the list of inhibiting effects that insulate management from the demands of the marketplace, and ask yourself whether these are potential problems for you. Take a couple of the most important decisions that your business makes, and ask yourself how they perform at each of the four phases of the OODA loop. Perhaps even administer a few of the questions from our survey (see appendix 2) to different levels of your company and see what the results are across levels and across regions.

Finally, begin to think of the processes that drive information and learning as essentials to strategy, not add-ons at the end. Include in every strategy discussion an agenda item regarding how the strategy and key initiatives are tested, informed by market feedback, and updated.

We close with a few questions to ask about any business regarding design principle 3:

- Is speed of reaction a competitive advantage for you? How do you know?

- How are you set up to react to major threats to part of your business model?

- Are you investing enough in the next-generation business model, in testing and experimenting in search of it?

- Do you track over time the rate of productivity improvement in core processes across the company (e.g., experience curve)? Should you?

- What are your most important types of decisions regarding change and adaptation? Is the process informed, clear, and simple? What are inhibitors?

We have now described the three design principles of Great Repeatable Models. We believe that these three principles should be a new standard for business strategy in the world of constant change that we inhabit. But it is not easy. We turn now to some of the archetypal challenges and trade-offs that CEOs face in trying to use these ideas, and in trying to make their company simpler, more transparent, and more responsive.

Leadership: Freedom or Framework?

In 1865, German physicist Rudolph Clausius coined the term *entropy* in his research on mechanical theories of heat. He used the concept to give a mathematical footing to the second law of thermodynamics, which states that without the injection of free energy, all systems tend to move from order to disorder. Entropy is all around us. Leonardo da Vinci's *The Last Supper*, which covers an end wall of the dining hall at the monastery of Santa Maria delle Grazie in Milan, began flaking within a few years of its completion; within sixty years, da Vinci's biographer referred to it as "ruined" (and this before a doorway was cut into it in the 1650s). Human systems tend even faster toward chaos. Just think of a roomful of schoolchildren at their desks ten minutes after the teacher leaves.

In business, entropy often leads to waste and loss of focus in the daily operations of complex organizations, such as the emergence of self-contained internal activities without direct linkage to, or value for, the customer. Yet, when organizations grow and become more complex, internal units proliferate. What began as a simple organizational structure becomes a matrix, or a complex cube, with separate geographical, functional, and product managers. Each has a staff, and each has facilitators to manage the interactions at the nodes of the cube. As the forces of entropy strengthen, more time is taken up with internal meetings, or written reports, or preoccupation with narrow, often political, agendas that come with complex organizational structures. The customer becomes less central and suffers, and the strategic priorities become less clear.

Entropy is the enemy of repeatable models, which, without strong management, can move from order to disorder. Think back to the case of Nokia that we introduced in chapter 1. The leaders of this company created a repeatable formula for tablet-shaped handsets that allowed Nokia to create enormous economies of scale and dominate its market for over a decade. Yet, despite enormous surplus resources during this time, the company's leaders failed to adapt and invest aggressively enough in the future. As a result, in just a year, Nokia lost its market position to Apple, Google, and Research in Motion. This lesson is all the more sobering given that Nokia's own R&D and product development teams had created many years earlier some of the basic concepts that were later used in the iPhone (large display, touch screen, Internet readiness, and an apps store).

Nokia is not alone. Kodak failed to respond effectively to the threat of digital photography despite being the leader in the technology. The Great Atlantic & Pacific Tea Company (A&P), a once dominant U.S. grocer, failed to respond to the threat of new store formats. Blockbuster was positioned to jump on the download wave before Netflix. Microsoft's Windows operating system was one of the great repeatable assets ever to build a company around, yet today the company is still anchored in the architecture of a product that many feel has inhibited its ability to "zero base" and adapt to new devices and to Web-based innovation. Even Dell, often cited as the greatest repeatable model of the 1990s in business, stalled out for a time, as it failed to adapt its model and eroded its competitive advantage when it let competitors catch up with its historic differentiation of low costs, low inventory, and fast service.

Entropy in business, unlike examples from the natural world, does not usually occur due to an absence of opportunity or impending obsolescence, according to our research. In fact, the 377 executives whom we surveyed in conjunction with the Economist Intelligence Unit saw opportunities everywhere, despite their enormous anxiety regarding the challenges of growth: 50 percent cited "tremendous opportunity" in the North American market, 65 percent in Europe, and more than 85 percent in Asia.[1] Only 15 percent of those surveyed said their growth was inhibited by lack of opportunities (see figure 5-1). Yet, virtually all were concerned with internal inhibitors to

FIGURE 5-1

Key barriers to growth cited by executives

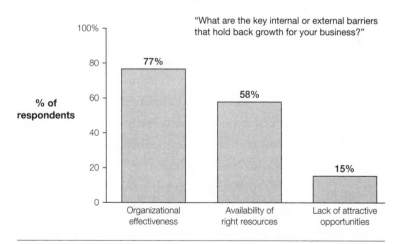

Note: Organizational effectiveness includes, for example, ability to focus, culture, and right business plans; availability of right resources includes both number and quality of resources/capabilities available.
Source: Bain/EIU survey of 377 executives of large companies in North America, Europe, and Asia.

growth; more than 75 percent cited factors relating to organizational effectiveness, especially excess complexity, difficulty achieving sufficient focus, or a risk-averse culture.

So far we have not talked about the central role of the leader. We are not of the school of thought that everything tracks back to the leader alone; that is not the case with the Great Repeatable Models, many of which experienced a leadership rotation and maintained momentum. Yet, for reinforcing the primacy of the repeatable model, and taking actions to prevent entropy and disorder and loss of learning from setting in, the role of the leader is critical. Jim Collins defined *level 5 leadership* in his book *Good to Great*, which looked at eleven companies that shifted from long periods of "satisfactory underperformance" to renewal and excellence.[2] He defined level 5 leadership as the ability of a leader to balance humility and focus on building the details of the company (he uses the analogy of a watchmaker at one point), with a strong and rigorous determination to prevail regarding those few most important long-term goals. Interestingly, the eleven "good to great companies" in his research are almost all single-core businesses built around a clear repeatable model. Our conclusion is that the leader must be the custodian of our three design principles.

This chapter focuses on leadership behaviors that could help a CEO and the management team to sustain and adapt the repeatable models of their company, and to fight the natural forces of entropy that seek to stop them.

No single solution works for all companies. However, leaders of the Great Repeatable Model companies did a number of things consistently to balance the inherent tension between freedom and framework (see table 5-1) and became, as only the leader can, the personal guardians of the three design principles.

TABLE 5-1

Outline of this chapter

	Design principle 1: a well-differentiated core	Design principle 2: clear nonnegotiables	Design principle 3: closed-loop learning
Freedom	• Broad, generic strategy: "grand vision"	• Driving empowerment: "expander culture"	• Continuous change: "business ADHD"
versus	**versus**	**versus**	**versus**
Framework	• Narrow, specific strategy: "to-do list"	• Driving compliance: "contractor culture"	• Relentless focus: "preventing the future"
Leadership best practices	• Focus on what really matters • Ground strategy in company heritage	• Cocreate and communicate • Support through KPIs, rewards, etc.	• Create processes to force feedback • Build capabilities to experiment and adapt

Source: Bain & Company.

The CEO as Guardian of Design Principle 1: A Well-Differentiated Core

The first design principle of Great Repeatable Models is a well-differentiated core business and a robust activity system to replicate it. Yet, as soon as a new strategy is defined, the forces of entropy set in. For instance, the organization can begin to lose focus on the specifics of differentiation if it is left at too high a level. Unless the strategy strongly highlights the few activities that really matter the most, the danger will be that nothing matters very much or everything matters a little bit. Vagueness and indecisiveness are the handmaidens of entropy. They lead to loss of discipline, to inconsistency, to ineffective learning, and ultimately to costly diseconomies of scale.

As organizations become more complex, forces appear that conspire to reduce the specificity in strategy, to ensure that all are included, and as a result, sharp choices become increasingly difficult to enforce. It may be "all about customer service," but leaders don't want to communicate this because it might alienate other parts of the organization, especially non-customer-facing functions. Loss of an ability to set sharp, focused priorities can erode the core of a once successful repeatable model.

Take, for example, the damage caused by many of the "customer excellence" programs over the last ten years. These programs were originally intended to revive a company's customer focus. But as we've seen with many of the companies we meet with as coheads of Bain's Global Strategy Practice, these programs were applied to all functions, regardless of whether the functions were actually customer facing. The result in many situations was more units with their own agendas, rising internal costs, and rampant complexity. We know of one company that has installed a global marketing department across its business units. However, the frontline employees at the local sales and marketing organizations in most cases don't appreciate the "help" they get; they feel held back by all the guidelines issued by "corporate." It has become a constant source of tension and cost, and has, ironically, made the company more internally focused.

One study on team performance looked at a sample of meetings, counting the "utterances" and classifying them as internal or external. The teams in the best-performing organizations had external focus in more than 70 percent of their comments, whereas the worst-performing teams were the reverse.[3] Entropy for the first design principle happens when a potentially well-differentiated core drifts toward vagueness due to these internal forces constantly battling for their own importance. For instance, without strong leadership around the first design principle, investment funds become spread more and more uniformly—some executives refer to it with the verb "peanut buttered"—across multiple activities and not ruthlessly focused on what matters the most.

Entropy can also occur in another way—when detailed instructions proliferate, and frontline activities become about filling in the checklist. The team stops thinking about the model from an external perspective and becomes internally focused, temporarily shielded by the economics of the original repeatable model. Eventually, the organization stops learning, becomes complacent, and stops adapting.

A good example of this is A&P, the once great retailer. The company was originally founded in 1859 as a tea company, selling tea by mail order from an office in New York. This led to retail outlets and, in 1912, to the introduction of a grocery format. This format was a brilliant repeatable model—by using the same format as it expanded, the company was able to reduce costs while increasing service levels. It grew to sixteen hundred stores by 1915, and a decade and a half later it had grown almost ten times. By the 1950s, it was the dominant food retailer in the United States, but then it steadily declined for the next twenty years (see figure 5-2). In December 2010, it filed for Chapter 11 bankruptcy protection. What went wrong?

FIGURE 5-2

The rise and fall of the Great Atlantic & Pacific Tea Company (A&P)

A&P sales (in 2010 constant dollars)

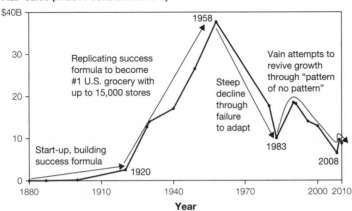

Sources: Company data, literature search.

Every rise-and-fall story has multiple root causes. But one thing that clearly went wrong with A&P during the '60s and '70s was that it did not adapt to new competition—it defined its repeatable model too narrowly and was too internally focused. In his book *How the Mighty Fall*, Jim Collins describes A&P's strategy during this era:

> When George Hartford, the leader who drove the extraordinary rise of A&P, lay on his deathbed in 1957, he summoned his longtime loyal aide, Ralph Burger, and pleaded as his dying wish, "Take care of the organization." . . . Burger, himself nearly seventy years old, spent decades as a chief confidant and pursued his solemn oath to preserve and protect the Hartford legacy with fundamentalist zeal . . . Insulated by A&P's comfortable position as the largest retailing organization in the world, Burger believed that "taking care of the organization" meant preserving its specific practices and methods; as late as 1973, Mr. John [Hartford]'s office remained exactly as it had been two decades earlier, right down to the same coat hangers hanging in the same place in the closet . . . During the Burger era, A&P's arrogant stance that "we will continue to keep things just the way they are and we will continue to be successful because—well, we're A&P!" left it vulnerable to new store formats developed by companies like Kroger.[4]

The impact of this failure to adapt is clear from figure 5-2: in a mere twenty-five years, A&P declined from the number one grocery chain to a marginal player, just a quarter of its former size.

You could argue that a retailer can be successful only as long as its specific model appeals to customers, and therefore A&P's model from a foregone era was doomed to fail anyway, regardless of management. This, however, doesn't appear to be true. Just consider the successes of retail companies like IKEA (1943), Publix

Super Markets (1930), Carrefour (1959), Tesco (1919), and Kroger (1883). All are retailers that have been able to stand the test of time and adapt their model to the changes the retail industry has faced over the past century. There doesn't appear to be any reason why A&P wouldn't have been able to do that with the right leadership.

In 1980, A&P replaced its executive team and careened "guard-rail to guardrail" toward the other end of the differentiation trap. Where under Burger everything had to stay the same, now nothing was sacred anymore. A&P went on a bold path of vigorous growth. Within a decade, it acquired Stop & Shop in New Jersey, Kohl's and Farmer Jack in the Great Lakes area; launched a new Super Fresh banner in Philadelphia; and went into Canada through the acquisition of Dominion—to mention just a few of the many initiatives pursued as part of its new "grand vision." Unsurprisingly, this "pattern of no pattern"—very much unlike its Great Repeatable Model of the past—failed to create any value, and soon A&P had to close and divest stores again to keep afloat.

In the next two decades, A&P retreated from the South and then expanded into discount grocery retailing, only to abandon it again a few years later in a major restructuring that also closed its business in Canada, Wisconsin, and New England. In a final attempt to grow, A&P acquired the Pathmark chain in 2007. The acquisition burdened A&P with a heavy debt load, forcing it to file for Chapter 11 bankruptcy protection a few years later.

This example clearly shows both extremes of the tension that leaders need to balance: defining the model too broadly versus defining it too narrowly. If a well-defined strategy is translated over time into a robotic checklist, it will disempower the organization and may even lead to efforts to protect the model instead of adapting it to new challenges. Alternatively, if the strategy is too broadly defined (as management shies away from tough choices), the organization will fill the vacuum, pursuing a blizzard of ever-changing activities and programs.

We highlight two specific actions that CEOs and the management team might reflect on in their custodianship of differentiation.

The Power of a Simple Focus

The first is to ensure that the strategy is absolutely grounded in the few essential actions that drive the company to both (a) leadership economics and (b) improved customer advocacy. The reason for this is simple. As shown in our book *Profit from the Core*, companies that achieve sustainable profitable growth create leadership economics in one or a few focused core businesses and have twice the level of customer advocacy as followers in their industry (see figure 5-3).[5] Of course, how you achieve these will differ greatly—just recall the vast differences between the models of IKEA, Enterprise Rent-A-Car, and Danaher. But the essential activities you must hardwire into the front line

FIGURE 5-3

Sustained value creators create leadership economics and loyal customers

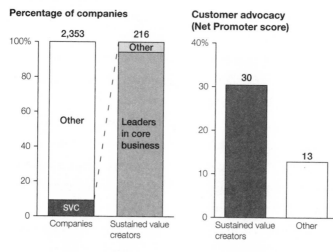

Sources: Worldscope; Bain analysis.

have the same purpose: to achieve leadership economics in the core of your business and to strive for superior customer loyalty relative to that of competitors.

Consider Julian Metcalfe, founder of Pret A Manger, the very successful U.K. sandwich shop built on the idea of freshly made, high-quality prepackaged sandwiches. At its essence, Pret's stated strategy was "fast service with a smile." That was it. This seemingly innocuous simple differentiation forced a whole series of decisions. It meant that the service menu needed to be simple so the staff could serve it quickly and reliably. At one point, the founder was challenged on Pret's lack of made-to-order sandwiches. Metcalfe responded, "If you want to make a sandwich in front of someone, and have our sort of volumes, then you need a line about a mile long. You can't keep people waiting a quarter of an hour. I can't bear queues. They mean unhappy customers and stressed staff," which clearly would go against the company's strategy.[6]

Through its concept of the Golden Rule, the Four Seasons hotel chain has fully hardwired its strategy into its frontline activities. And these frontline activities are the essential ones that matter, that "wow the customer" with extraordinary service. Founder and chairman Isadore Sharp describes the principle's importance: "I sat down with our communications experts and wrote down the fundamentals of our culture, which is based on the Golden Rule—to treat others as you wish to be treated."[7] Elsewhere, he adds, "'The Golden Rule' is at the heart of our operating principles, and is part of every aspect of our business. Hotel staff is empowered to serve guests by making instant decisions, guided by the idea that one should treat others as one would be treated. Executives are similarly empowered, and with empowerment comes responsibility . . . we are all personally accountable for our role in the company's success."[8]

The Golden Rule is baked into all of the company's training programs, including the "familiarization day," where employees are invited as guests to the hotel to experience the other side of service delivery. Says Ellen Dubois du Bellay, vice president of learning and development, "They're learning what it looks like to receive service from the other side."[9] Note that the Golden Rule covers one thing: customer-facing roles. It hardwires differentiation into frontline activity that drives leadership and customer advocacy.

If the CEO is able to hardwire frontline activities that deliver real differentiation to the customer, the customers and front lines will propel a positive and self-reinforcing cycle. Customer feedback improves. Sales improve. The lives of those on the front line improve. As Paul Polman, CEO of Unilever, says, "I go to a lot of home visits or go around with shoppers, and I've seldom met a consumer who buys our wonderful Knorr products or Lipton or Omo or Skippy because they like our strategy. And so, once we have set our strategy in the company, our business becomes a very simple one of getting the right products at the right place at the right quality at the right price—all the time."[10]

Link the Future to Past Greatness

The second observation from successful guardians of the soul of a repeatable model is that they maintain a keen sense of the company's history and an ability to use it while communicating the elements of strategy. Sometimes, the repeatable model of today is rooted in "rediscovery" of lost differentiation. Recall from chapter 2 how LEGO CEO Jørgen Vig Knudstorp led the company's recovery by reaching back to its founding principles. He "rediscovered the brick." "[Our turnaround] was rebuilding the company piece by piece," says Knudstorp. "But it was building a different company that was faithful to LEGO's past."[11] "The heritage is extremely important," he adds.[12]

Paul Polman of Unilever describes the role of history in helping him strike this balance in his attempt to renew one of the world's iconic companies:

> You must root the strategy in the history of the company. Don't talk about changing everything. People join and stay with companies because they are very proud of that company's history, traditions, and its ways of working. You can't suddenly tell all those who have joined a company they were proud of, and all those in charge of that company, that everything is suddenly wrong. Firstly, that is never true, and certainly not in the case of Unilever. But secondly, even if it were somewhat true, that is too demoralizing. I always talked about the change as rediscovering the greatness of our history. With a company as rich in history and success as Unilever, you can find incredible examples of previous greatness for almost every ambition you have. I became obsessed with the company's history and was always able to find some moment of brilliant excellence to back up and illustrate the ambitions that we put in place. We weren't driving change through destruction; we drove change through rediscovery. That is very different indeed.[13]

All Great Repeatable Models we studied focused on a few core sources of differentiation—shunning the "idée du jour" for time-honored fundamentals of business economics. Peter Drucker, too, has written about how distractions can so easily lead to entropy in companies that are sloppy about maintaining simplicity and single-mindedness of focus: "Typically such a business goes in for the latest management fads. When 'human relations' are in season, it hires psychologists, social workers, and personnel experts and puts everyone through 'leadership training.' Two years later everybody talks 'operations research' and attends management-science seminars."[14]

The CEO as Guardian of Design Principle 2: Clear Nonnegotiables

The second design principle focuses on nonnegotiables, a relatively short and strong list of rules to guide the key behaviors and decisions that are most central to the strategy and the differentiation that propels it. The nonnegotiables help to create organizational alignment around the set of things "we all believe in and agree to do."

Defining the level of specificity of the nonnegotiables in a way that fits with the strategy and with the culture of the company is a challenge of leadership. Consider a simple illustration based on two contrasting company cultures—"the expanders" versus "the contractors" (see table 5-2). The expander culture is characterized on the positive side by extreme entrepreneurialism, innovation, adaptation, and flexibility. On the negative side, expanders can be undisciplined and prone to reinvent the wheel, creating complexity. As guardians of nonnegotiables, CEOs of expanders need to ensure that nonnegotiables are defined quite specifically, leaving little room for interpretation on the really important things, while finding ways to allow for the natural creativity of the organization to be fulfilled and channeled in a focused way. Think of Google, which has clear core principles and focus, but also is made up of brilliant software engineers who can and want to invent the future. If nonnegotiables are left too vague, expanders will interpret the strategy and its essentials in a wide variety of ways.

A CEO in a contractor culture faces an opposite problem. On the positive side, contractors are extremely disciplined, execution oriented, and intolerant of ambiguity. But they are also prone to be overly process oriented and inflexible and would rather work from rule books and checklists. Contractors take a small set of nonnegotiables and turn them into a long checklist, each with multiple key performance indicators (KPIs). Contractors create "compliance" matrices to monitor performance against the checklists. Innovation can be stifled, and the company's ability to adapt can be severely hampered. Here, the CEO must make sure that the nonnegotiables don't degenerate into a set of rule books, by working to highlight over and over the core principles. Culture matters. As the former head of HR at Unilever, Sandy Ogg, often says, "Strategy and culture both matter, but absent true leadership, culture will win every time."[15]

David Haines, CEO of Grohe, explains the challenge of developing nonnegotiables in a contractor culture. Founded in 1936, when Friedrich Grohe took over Berkenhoff & Paschedag, Grohe is the world's leading premium faucet company. Haines has driven a strategy focused on maintaining its premium positioning, by combining the company's core skills in manufacturing innovation, and water technologies. Having experienced

TABLE 5-2

The dilemma of nonnegotiables: contractors versus expanders culture

	Contractors	Expanders
Think of a . . .	German midsize engineering firm	Professional services partnership
Culture	Hierarchical: do what the boss says	Entrepreneurial: endless frontline adaptation
Impact of entropy	Turning into a bureaucracy governed by rules and guidelines	Increasing complexity as established routines deteriorate
The task of the leader	Empower the front line by establishing goals and driving ownership of them	Align the organization on a few common "all of us, all the time" behaviors
Role of nonnegotiables	Provide goals rather than rules and checklists	Align on a few specific routines to foster experience sharing

Source: Bain & Company.

multiple private equity owners over several years and gone through its share of cost cutting, the organization had become less focused on growth and innovation. Haines explains:

> I wanted to refocus the organization on growth, which started with great innovation. I wanted our people to believe in our products, in their superiority and in our leadership of the premium segment. I wanted them to explain with pride why the trade and consumer should pay more for our products versus cheaper Chinese imports. I recognized that our strategy was not simply to be differentiated, but also to be able to empower our front line to explain our differentiation and have pride in it. But I also knew we were a typical German midsized company, with very loyal management. They would execute our strategy in detail regardless of whether they believed in it. I didn't want that. I needed them to believe, and therefore it was far more important to align on general principles about how we were differentiated. I had no worries my organization would implement, following through on every detail. My worry was they would do it without believing, without question. So we launched the Grohe "Moments of Truth" initiative, where we worked with our employees to set out why our products were better. The fact was, our products were far better than the competition but we lost the art of explaining why.[16]

An example of a moment of truth for Grohe is Grohe CoolTouch technology, which demonstrates that a Grohe faucet doesn't get hot, even if hot water passes through it for long periods of time. Grohe StarLight technology discusses the quality of chrome finishes that are resistant to water stains. Haines's goal was to drive a strategy of product superiority into a set of nonnegotiables—but he did so "with the grain of the culture," not against it.

How, then, do CEOs act as guardians of nonnegotiables, our second design principle? We draw attention to two practices.

Drive Cocreation

The first action employs a well-defined process of cocreation to involve people across the business in articulating, refining, and applying the nonnegotiables to their job. Remember the story in chapter 3 of how DaVita created its nonnegotiables? If you take another look at that story, you'll see just how important a role was played by Kent Thiry, who initiated the process despite skepticism on the part of his fellow executives. Without Thiry, the company might have focused on stabilizing its finances and would have missed the tremendous culture-building opportunity its crisis had presented and that turned out to be central to its ultimate durability. He engaged actively with the front line, leading a series of town hall meetings around creating a new set of values and principles for the business. Thiry began to communicate directly through e-mails and blogs with managers at all levels, reducing the distance enormously between the new CEO and the embittered front line. Through these behaviors, he sent a powerful signal about the importance of the nonnegotiables.

Another powerful example of cocreation is Unilever. As a new CEO, Paul Polman created what he called the CEO Forum, made up of the leaders of all key markets and categories. He worked with them actively over the course of a full year to establish and propel a set of nonnegotiables in a company that was once voted as the most complex company on earth. This set of principles fed into the strategy of the firm on a single page, which he refers to as Unilever's Compass.

Get the Strategy on a Page

After the nonnegotiables have been cocreated, the next step is to communicate so that the whole organization can engage with the repeatable model. CEOs refer to *the slide*, or to *a strategy on a page*. It is how key meetings begin and end—one-on-ones, town halls, or investor presentations. It sets out simply and clearly the source of differentiation and the choices of where to play and how to win (see figure 5-4). As Paul Polman says, "We are well aware of the need to create sustainable top and bottom line growth, which is why we launched what we call 'the Compass' in 2009. The Compass is an energizing vision and strategy to bring the company back to sustainable growth. It puts growth, based on a passion for the consumer and customer, firmly back on the agenda. The vision we set ourselves is to double the business and outperform market growth, whilst at the same time reducing our overall environmental impact."[17]

FIGURE 5-4

Pyramid to develop a "strategy on a page"

- A good strategy on a page begins with a clear articulation of the company's ambition, which should be bold, specific, and inspiring, and target sustained, profitable growth.

- Choices on where to play and how to win follow from the ambition. These choices take into account a deep understanding of the company's core, and where it should focus, expand, and redefine its business(es). They also aim to win with the customer and beat the competition in a repeatable way. Nonnegotiable principles determine how the company will win.

- The strategy then needs to be translated into specific actions that reflect differential resourcing and capability building to win.

- No strategy is complete without embedding how it will achieve lasting results. This includes building the organizational capacity to execute, mobilizing frontline pull for change, and integrating fast feedback loops for adaptation.

Source: Bain & Company.

The slide must be simple. As Gareth Penny, former CEO of De Beers describes it, "The role of a CEO is to simplify the complexity and stick to a few themes that are easy to understand, [and] can cascade to a few KPIs [that] are easy to communicate. A CEO must boil away the complexity to get issues to their essence."[18] David Haines, the CEO of Grohe, talks about the CEO as the great "disaggregator": "Management teams working in complex organizations competing in complex markets will eventually agree that everything is too complicated to deal with. The CEO must intervene and be the one that disaggregates the problem into solvable pieces. If we aren't the voice of simplicity, who will be?"[19]

Link Nonnegotiables to Rewards

The CEO can also shape rewards as a way to strengthen the force of the nonnegotiables of the strategy. The Enterprise Rent-A-Car operating model provides an example. In chapter 3 we described ESQi, which measures the percentage of completely satisfied Enterprise customers. Andy Taylor, the CEO, describes how the company linked this "customer nonnegotiable" to career progression: "All people's promotability is based upon their customer satisfaction scores, the ESQi."[20] If the branch is below the corporate target in customer scores, no one in that branch gets promoted. Taylor continues, "The field named it 'ESQi jail.' What it really means is that you are not at or above corporate average in your completely satisfied percentage, and every one of our 7,000 branches are measured individually with a statistically valid sample of customers. Our corporate average right now is about 79 percent of our customers completely satisfied, and so if you are at 77 percent in your branch for instance, you're not in the promotion pool."[21]

During the turnaround of Gucci, one of the first acts of CEO Robert Polet was to shift P&L accountability away from the center and back to the brands, which were given almost full autonomy as long as they complied with a set of nonnegotiables. In exchange for more autonomy regarding actions they could take in their market, the brand leaders cosigned a two-page document with Polet, agreeing on the trade-offs and decisions that had to be elevated up the chain of command.[22] He made sure the organization structure matched what he was trying to do with brands, which was to make the brand the "hero" again. He described his intention as follows: "I want the people to work in what I call freedom within the framework. They need to feel responsible, that they have the freedom to follow their instincts, intuitions, and own way of working. But they also need to know that there are limits they cannot trespass, like betraying the brand's DNA."[23]

Create Champions and Heroes

Great guardians of the second design principle can also highlight local heroes and champions of certain behaviors—people who embody and believe in the most important principles across the organization. Change management experts at our companies always emphasize the central role in driving new behavior by what they call a "supporter spine" of advocates of the change—a spine that forms an unbroken chain from top to bottom. During change programs to revise a strategy or reintroduce the essentials of a repeatable model, they even recommend mapping this out explicitly at the level of the individual person.

Paul Polman at Unilever holds annual Compass Awards to recognize the heroes who best live the spirit of the Compass. As he explains, "We have kept the drumbeat on increasing the pace of the organization and of becoming more consumer centric. On every initiative, we 'found the hero' who got results from that initiative and improved the lives of the consumer or customer. The stories of those heroes have become legends and are spread around the company. We cascaded communications endlessly, from the Executive Team to the CEO Forum, to the Change Leaders conference, to our global team at the front line."[24]

Indeed, we have found that more than 90 percent of companies satisfied with their financial performance believe that "culture is as important as strategy for business successes."[25] Truly understanding that culture, and its natural tendency toward freedom or framework, is critical to customizing the right approach to the strategic nonnegotiables that will "pull" the strategy throughout the organization.

The CEO as Guardian of Design Principle 3: Closed-Loop Learning

The third design principle is shaped by the increased importance of feedback loops and adaptation in creating lasting businesses. The CEO role as guardian here is perhaps the hardest of all as he must balance the need for absolute focus with the need for relatively frequent change. It is not surprising that this area was rated as the most difficult in our data and surveys, and that there are numerous examples of where the best-performing businesses during one period foundered, for exactly this reason, during the next period.

An excellent example of a leader who dealt with the balance of focus and adaptability is Nicky Oppenheimer, the executive chairman of De Beers, the world's leading diamond trader and diamond jewelry brand. The company was named after the De Beers farm where the huge diamond deposits at Kimberley, in South Africa, were found. Heritage and legacy are everything for a company where leadership has been handed down from Ernest Oppenheimer, who took control of the company in 1927, to his son Harry, and finally to Harry's son, Nicky.

One cause of De Beers's success during the three generations of Oppenheimers was the company's unbroken and relentless attention to its core strategy of focusing on diamond supply, enhanced further by investment in innovative marketing campaigns that reinforced the mystique of diamonds. In fact, its "diamonds are forever" campaign was named the most powerful advertising slogan of the last century by *Advertising Age* magazine. De Beers's original repeatable model was once so powerful that it captured for more than one hundred years overwhelming market share in rough diamonds mined and sold in the world. But all good things come to an end in business. Its Great Repeatable Model hit a wall in the 1990s as De Beers's influence on diamond production declined and reduced its market share by about half with the rise of Russian, Australian, and Canadian mines, compounded by a softening in the gem market. To manage a supply-focus strategy even further, while defending the business model of the past, De Beers built an economically unsustainable stockpile of natural diamonds, valued at more than $5 billion.

Something had to change. After a major strategic review of its model, the company was left with two options: try to restore its control over production or change the model completely to a more demand-driven one. This was put to a vote of the board and the management team. Just before the vote, Nicky Oppenheimer introduced the decision in front of the team: "When my father passed on leadership of the company to me, he gave me critical advice. 'Nicky,' he said, '99 percent of your job will be to preserve the legacy and strategy of De Beers. It is a great company and part of its greatness is, we've avoided changing to respond to new fads or opinions. But 1 percent of your job will be to know when it is time to change fundamentally and completely. Just be right when you exercise the 1 percent option, my son.'" Nicky Oppenheimer then looked at each of the members of his team and concluded, "I am convinced, this is that 1 percent moment and we need to change direction."[26] Two interesting things then happened. First, the vote carried overwhelmingly to adapt, to change the repeatable model. Second, the conference room in Kimberley where the meeting was held was immediately struck by lightning and lost power. Nicky rapidly interjected to close the meeting, "And I assume that is my father saying we made the right decision."[27] This moment is known now in De Beers as the "Kimberley lightning strike" and is used as an example of courageous leadership. But this 99 percent–1 percent moment, which is probably closer to 80 percent–20 percent in most companies, is the hardest act in business—when to focus, when to adapt. How can the leader simultaneously gain advantage from ruthless focus and endless adaptation?

We've found that the best guardians of the third design principle, all in their own way, rely on two types of leadership actions, maintaining focus on the core business while at the same time forcing it to adapt to changing conditions.

Own the Learning Process

The CEO needs to be seen as the companywide owner of the process by which external feedback leads to decisions around focus versus adaptation of the repeatable model. The CEO must champion this as no one else can, for it is critical to sustainability of the business.

Let's return to the leadership of Enterprise. CEO Andy Taylor did a number of things to shape the operating model of the company in a way that achieved a balance of consistency and adaptation. First, he was the "voice of the customer" and the "voice of the front line" in everything he did. Through his focus on developing customer advocates and tying all rewards in the company to increasing satisfaction scores, he reduced the complexity of his business—he shortened the time and distance between the customer, the front line, and the leadership team. Customer feedback was collected on a daily basis and executed fully on a weekly basis. He established a rhythm where the repeatable model of Enterprise was challenged and adapted weekly—in fact, the power of adaptation became a key competitive weapon.

Recall our earlier discussion of the transformation of Vodafone into a global leader. During this growth period, a time of enormous turbulence and dynamics in the industry, Chris Gent forced adaptation into the Vodafone model through the Brocket Hall process. Each year he brought his full team together to review changes in the mobile phone industry and determine the actions Vodafone should take to adapt. He explains, "Once a year we essentially dismantled our business system completely, investigating all major changes in the competitive and customer environment. We then decided together, as a management team, how to build it back up to compete over the next year. During these meetings, I allowed any and all issues to be raised and debated, but in exchange, for the rest of the year, I wanted my management team to focus on execution.[28]

"These sessions often raised serious challenges to Vodafone's repeatable model, leading to long debates that might otherwise not have taken place about when it was appropriate to adapt versus continue with the current model.[29]

"Most of the time, we were better off sticking to our knitting. We had built our model off our U.K. business and found that it worked incredibly well as we rolled it out to Germany, to Greece, and other markets in Europe. In Italy, the market and regulatory structure were completely different, and after rigorous debate we correctly decided not to apply the model there."[30]

Gent also emphasizes the importance of culture in forcing real debate about focus versus adaptation: "The Brocket Hall issues were never easy, and the choices we made involved winners and losers in our business. In all debates, we encouraged our leadership to wear a Vodafone hat, not the hat of the function or market they represented. This is easier said than done, but requires a huge amount of trust. We only succeeded because we invested as much time aligning around our shared vision and values as we did debating 'focus versus adapt' strategy issues."[31]

The most successful teams at the helm of the Great Repeatable Model companies turn the debate on adaptation into a competitive weapon—forcing continual discussion of changing market dynamics. They own the process and don't let feedback become a free-for-all. Either they control it through the daily rhythm of the business, as Andy Taylor did, or they set aside the time and space to debate changes to the repeatable model, as Gent did. Discipline, even over change, rules.

Culturally, this starts with a very simple norm around courageous leadership, in contrast with common organizational behaviors that "fight the future." Let's return to the Kodak story. A number of myths surround the Kodak meltdown. One myth is that the senior leadership of Kodak did not anticipate the arrival of digital photography, had their heads in the sand, and ultimately were blindsided by a new value proposition that was better than traditional film. The reality was, at the start of digital photography Kodak was the world leader in the field. In fact, years before it happened, Kodak management was able to predict accurately the moment that digital and traditional photography would be equal and digital would begin to take significant share (measured as the moment that a digital camera cost the same as a traditional camera to produce the same quality 5" by 7" photo).[32] Kodak also had a fantastic brand proposition for the digital world, leveraging its brand values of helping consumers reliably capture, store, and share their best memories. At issue, however, was that at every moment, from a near-term financial perspective, it was always the better decision for shareholders to fight the future—that is, continue to promote traditional film as long as possible. With a brand as important as Kodak, a rapid move and an endorsement of digital would accelerate consumer moves from traditional film. This was not bad management putting its head in the sand; this was simply management trying to preserve economic value and responding to incentives.

And that is the ultimate challenge of adaptation: it is expensive. Given that, it can easily feel better to fight adaptation, ride the core business a little longer, and hit short-term earnings targets. We studied forty cases (see figure 5-5) of companies that had repeatable models that eroded and stalled out. Of these, well over 60 percent were a result of losing focus on the core. This is why most managers are, and should be, biased to stay focused on the core—because losing focus explains so many failures.

However, sometimes, a pure focus on past success can lead to a management team that is constantly trying to "prevent the

FIGURE 5-5

Most stall-outs are due to loss of focus, and very few recover

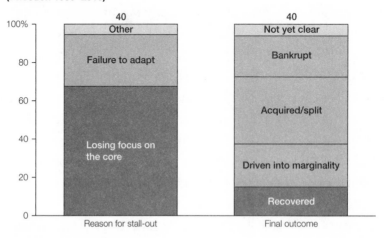

Percentage of stall-outs
(selection 1980–2010)

Sources: Company data; literature search.

future." That explains why one-third of stall-outs occur because of failure to adapt. And in many cases, the companies that failed to adapt did have the position and resources to adapt their business model had they reacted quickly. Avoiding what everyone else really knows, or senses, destroys organizations and confidence in their leaders. The CEO must lead and force debate about adaptation early, because only the CEO can endorse a move that, from a pure near-term economic perspective, gives the initial impression of destroying value, when it is really adapting a repeatable model so it can continue to repeat in the inevitable future.

Our research is revealing here. Senior executives of the lowest-performing companies are three times more likely to argue that "day-to-day battles" prevent them from stepping back and looking at business fundamentals. And they are also three times more likely to say they don't confront challenges to their business model (see figure 5-6). The enemy of adaptation

FIGURE 5-6

Executives' ability to step back and confront their true challenges

Percentage of respondents by performance

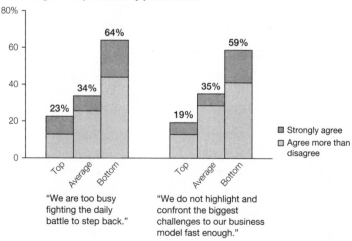

"We are too busy fighting the daily battle to step back."

"We do not highlight and confront the biggest challenges to our business model fast enough."

■ Strongly agree
□ Agree more than disagree

Source: Bain/EIU survey with 377 executives of large companies.

is day-to-day firefights and near-term profit pressures. This is all the more important given that our research also suggests that the requirements for adaptation have doubled in the last twenty years. In an analysis of the *Fortune* 500 we did for our book *Unstoppable*, we found that while 50 percent of large companies experienced no real change in their core business over 1985–1995, fewer than 30 percent are likely to be stable over 2005–2014.[33]

Organizationally, the CEO must create the right balance between focus and adaptation. This often leads to the CEO encouraging more experimentation in the business. The most successful technology companies are very good at this, as Jeff Bezos, CEO of Amazon, explains:

> What you really want to do companywide is maximize the number of experiments you can do per given unit of time. If something's really big—like the big bet we've made on Amazon Web Services—then sure, you can do only a limited number of those, so you spend more time thinking about them and talking them through. Somebody wears the black hat and makes the case for why not to do it, and somebody else puts on the white hat and says why it is actually a good thing to do. But since the outcomes of all these things are uncertain, if you can figure out how to conduct an experiment, you can make more bets. So the key, really, is reducing the cost of the experiments.[34]

But this is also true in more traditional businesses. IKEA's founder, Ingvar Kamprad, talks about the need to experiment and tolerate mistakes: "Only while sleeping one makes no mistakes. Making mistakes is the privilege of the active—of those who can correct their mistakes and put them right. There are few people who have made so many fiascos in my life as I have."[35]

Few CEOs will face the "lighting strike" moment experienced by the leadership team of De Beers. But all will face the need to balance continual focus on sustaining the existing business *and* continually adapting it to new challenges. Leaders ensure they have the external feedback to know when it is time to change. And great leaders have the courage to change even when the near-term impact is high. Reflecting on the Brocket Hall process, Chris Gent noted, "Looking back, I'm not sure of a decision that we took too soon. Unfortunately, there's a longer list of decisions that we took too late. No matter how 'bold' adaptation is at the time, it is almost always true you're too late."[36]

It Starts with Leadership

A lasting repeatable model needs the CEO and an enthusiastic management team to be the custodian of our three design principles and to manage the three tensions that we have described in this chapter. CEOs of Great Repeatable Model companies need to ensure the existence of a high-level strategic vision for the company but also take charge of a few of the key elements of the strategy to drive to the front line and change behaviors. Repeatable models require the management team to agree to a set of "all of us, all the time" activities that can be measured and tracked. The CEO must ensure, though, that these nonnegotiables empower the front line rather than constrain it. Finally, the CEO must manage a balancing act—ensuring that there is a constant drumbeat of demands to adapt and embellish the model while creating a process that focuses adaptation on the critical few. These three balancing acts are all different aspects of imposing "freedom within a framework." None are easy. Yet, the benefits can be huge—less complexity, more energy, and better connectedness between the CEO and the front line, and then between the front line and the customer.

Unfortunately, such leadership is not that common, which is a factor in why 90 percent of companies fail to hit their growth targets on a sustained basis and more than 80 percent of stall-outs were avoidable.[37] Just look at Citigroup's disastrous "financial supermarket" strategy and Time Warner's attempt to define *new media* through the merger with AOL—the biggest, and arguably the most value-destroying, in American business history. Or think of Kodak's failure to respond to the digital threat—to quote former CTO Bill Lloyd, who had joined the company in 2003, "[they had] developed antibodies against anything that might compete with film."[38]

Repeatable models simplify, but if you let them weaken unduly, increasing complexity can set in. The outcome of our survey in conjunction with the Economist Intelligence Unit is telling in that respect: about half of the executives at the lowest-performing companies indicate that they have too many IT systems and that the complexity of their organizations makes it more difficult than ever to react fast enough.[39] Rather than reconnect the CEO to the front line and the front line to the customer, the cascade of management processes and IT systems increases the time and distance between the CEO and the customer. The customer ultimately loses out. Entropy is the enemy of repeatable models. Absent the right leadership, entropy wins every time.

6

The Triumph of Simplicity

A leader is never more in touch with the front line of a business than when the founding team (some combination of CEO, head of product, and head of sales) makes its first sale. At that point, the leaders are the front line, and the first sale to a customer is everything. In fact, the customer probably even helped to design the product and gives constant feedback on product performance and next-generation requirements.

But success breeds growth, and this growth moves leaders farther from the front line and from customers. Growth brings layers of management and complex matrix organizations, each cell having its own self-contained agenda. Growth brings complexity of service and product offerings, which can reduce consistency. Growth brings increasingly diverse customers with needs that are increasingly different from the original core. Growth brings more opportunities for even the simplest communication to become distorted up and down the chain of command. Complexity is the inevitable consequence of growth, and ultimately its silent killer.

One study reported in *Harvard Business Review* on the challenges of growth noted, "Very few factors help produce economies of scale. Technology may be one, but not people. When it comes to motivating people and using their brainpower, you hit *diseconomies* of scale early. At that point, bigger isn't better."[1] The customer suffers. The learning curve flattens out. The ability to adapt declines. Complexity has reared its head.

Yet, the answer is not simply to stay small. That is not usually sustainable. The prospect of growth keeps the smart up-and-comers in the company. In the long run, only (profitable) growth creates real economic value. Moreover, in most markets, if you are not gaining market share you are losing position, and that is bad. Unfortunately, perhaps, growth is usually a nonnegotiable of strategy in business. But if growth creates an equal and opposite rise of unconstructive complexity, then what?

We know of a number of companies that experienced a stall-out of organic growth due to complexity, did not attack (or even recognize) the root cause of the problem, but felt that it signaled time to shift its source of targeted growth, to grow by becoming innovative (leading to big ideation projects amid widespread frustration, or sometimes to further proliferation of product variations and complexity) or through acquisition. Yup, shift to buy your way out of the problem by purchasing other people's smaller, and perhaps growing, companies.

In these cases, an increasing number of acquisitions were made competently. Costs were reduced on target through scale purchasing advantages. Yet the hoped-for revenue boost (e.g., through better global distribution) never materialized. In fact, the newly acquired companies even started having similar problems as the new parent—a high complexity tax, payable on joining the company. Once-hot businesses filled with entrepreneurial energy started to lose their innovation edge, and slowed down. The first reaction? Ramp up acquisitions even faster. The eventual realization? We had better attack directly the curse of complexity.

This is the background against which the advantages of repeatable models in a world of constant change stand in sharp relief—and offer real relief—for businesses, the people who inhabit them, the customers who use them, and the companies in their ecosystem that must cooperate with them.

In this concluding chapter, we promise to follow our own suggestion and not to add undue complexity, but rather to do only two things. The first is to expand a bit more on the topic of complexity, perhaps the metatheme of this book, to summarize the competitive advantages and the basic human advantage when simplicity breaks out, triumphant. Finally, we summarize briefly the ten key findings from our research on barriers to growth and the power of Great Repeatable Models.

We hope that our choice of examples has demonstrated that the ideas that emerge from our work on repeatable models can help to improve the performance of start-ups, of successful companies interested in raising their game and becoming more enduring, and of some types of businesses that are facing stall-out. We do not put forth these ideas as a cure-all or as a life-giving elixir in the case of a business with no core strength to build on. However, we have found these ideas to be practical, effective, and robust in improving a wide range of business situations. We admit that we did feature some of the most iconic repeatable models, like IKEA or Vanguard, in order to illustrate the design principles and the benefits of repeatable models in their purest form. Surely, to learn to hit a tennis ball correctly, you will find great value from studying the footwork, discipline, preparation, and technique of Roger Federer even if you cannot aspire to his level of play.

The Real Cost of Complexity

The growth of complexity makes organizations confused about who the customer is. It can result in policies that treat customers as if they were some mythical "typical" customer. More insidiously, as back-office functions build up, the notion of the internal customer is introduced. *Customer* becomes a generic term that denotes "someone you need to serve," but little distinction is made between internal and external—and even externally, between the most valuable and least valuable. As a result, the organization becomes less attuned to the founder's principle that the customer is first. Sam Walton, the founder of Wal-Mart, said, "There is only one boss. The customer—and he can fire everybody in the company from the chairman on down, simply by spending his money somewhere else."[2] This clarity gets lost in organizations as they grow.

The front line also gets lost as the importance of the customer gets lost. The front line—sales, customer care, customer service, and so forth—becomes just another function. The frontline reporting of customer issues becomes no more important than any other function reporting on issues. In some organizations, the front line is perceived as the function protecting management from customer issues, such as complaints about poor service or product issues.

At its worst, customer interactions are confined to call centers, and these call centers are viewed as pure cost items to be managed down, or even to be outsourced to another company in a distant country. Frontline employees are turned into commodities to be traded around in search of the lowest cost. Just think of some of your recent frustrations as a consumer: getting lost in endless phone menus for a problem you have with a home service, only to be connected with a distant phone service representative who is rewarded by ending the conversation as soon as possible. One mobile operator commented to us, "How can you be customer oriented when those most accountable for serving customers are among the least influential in the company?" What an incredibly sad and wrong situation.

The farther leaders get from the front line, the harder it becomes to make decisions. In some large corporations we know, you now need months and multiple committees to actually complete a *decision cycle*—that is, the time from when a CEO makes a decision to offer something to a customer, through when it is designed and delivered and feedback is received, to when the proposition is adapted and reoffered. As mentioned earlier, past studies find a strong relationship between the ability to decide fast (faster than competitors) and success; and between the share of time in meetings devoted to internal agendas versus the customer and the market.

When the ability to decide bogs down, basic belief systems and respect for the leadership erode. The obsessive vision of the founder and the subsequent leadership team is watered down, often replaced by less inspiring, even bland prose, compromise, and ultimately mediocrity. When the edginess and energy source of the early years evaporates, the type of people who want to stay or work in the new environment poses yet another challenge to the company. Complexity dulls intensity and the sharpness of differentiation every time.

A central irony of the danger of complexity is that the financially healthiest businesses are often the most vulnerable. Management teams often treat these businesses as a "golden goose" that is not to be disturbed or pushed too hard. The frequent consequence is that the healthy business can languish, basking in a fantasy land of "satisfactory underperformance," while a distracted management becomes bored with the core and pursues new adventures (or usually misadventures). Our recently revised book, *Profit from the Core*, studies this phenomenon and is replete with examples of strong core businesses that lost their focus and market position due to such controllable factors.

Simplicity Makes You Healthier

The most lasting way to overcome creeping internal complexity, we believe, is to become more disciplined about simplicity. The design principles of the Great Repeatable Models are well suited to reduce organizational complexity, as is shown by many of the examples of rejuvenation that we looked at: think back to LEGO, DaVita, P&G, Hilti, and MSC. They help to bring leaders back to the front lines and make it easier for people throughout the organization to make coordinated and faster decisions.

External complexity of markets and customer needs is different because it can actually create opportunity to avoid commoditization. Such complexity creates opportunities for repeated creation of protected niches, it creates opportunities for switching costs at the customer, and it creates opportunities for "follow-on" service revenue streams. Olam, for example, operates across a wide range of products, activities, and geographies. Yet, it is this very network and market complexity that lets Olam identify hundreds of places to extend its repeatable positioning and capabilities—new geographies, new commodities, new processes, and new risk management services and other value added solutions. Technological complexity in markets creates opportunities for companies like Google to build substantial barriers to entry through superior software and switching costs, or companies like Novozymes to have a repeatable formula to create bioengineered industrial enzymes custom-designed with each customer. Having complex customers enables smart companies like Medtronic in medical implantable devices, or SAP in enterprise software to build customer loyalty, create switching costs, and raise competitive barriers.

The ability to take advantage of the *external complexity* of markets is made easier if you can control the self-induced *internal complexity* of your business model. Companies like Apple, with a short list of SKUs and consistent product characteristics, show the value of a simpler internal business model. Just look at the hundreds of thousands of applications for the iPhone and iPad that appeared rapidly, and seemingly out of nowhere, yet are completely accessible, organized, and consistent in how they can be acquired.

It's important for managers to distinguish these external complexities from the internal, organizational complexity that kills companies. It's a bit like the difference between good and bad cholesterol—both are similar in nature, but one promotes health and creates energy, while the other does the opposite.

Figure 6-1 shows the data from our executive survey with the Economist Intelligence Unit.[3] We separated the 377 responses

FIGURE 6-1

Design principles and low complexity reinforce each other

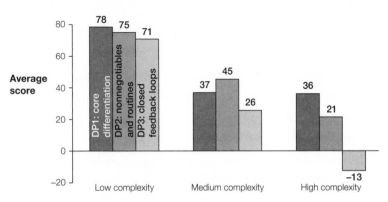

Source: Bain 200 Company Database of Repeatable Models.

according to perceived level of excess complexity in their organizations. You can see that the organizations perceived to be overly complex for their markets do not come close to adhering to the design principles of the Great Repeatable Models as much as the better-performing businesses do. A recent study by our colleagues defined relative complexity across paired competitors in different industries (with measures that differed by type of business). The least complex one-third outperformed the most complex one-third by an average of more than 10 percent annual rate of revenue growth, driving a much higher return on capital.

We have focused this discussion primarily on the organizational complexity that we find repeatable models can help to control. Yet, there are two other dimensions to consider.

One has its origins in the observation that more company strategies rely on other businesses and agents in an ecosystem of mutual dependence. The increasing importance of ecosystems in strategy has been studied by others, with common examples being companies like Wal-Mart, Google, Apple, and SAP.[4] Yet, interestingly, companies that are cited as examples of strategies that derive clear competitive advantage from their ability to weave a network and work with their ecosystem partners are also often found on our list of sustained value creators with single primary cores whose strategy is built around a well-defined repeatable model. Companies without clarity, transparency, and accessibility find it much harder to engage simply with other companies. Great Repeatable Model companies, on average, make better partners.

Finally, there is the ultimate inner game at the level of the individual employee. The typical employee has a working memory that can hold a list of about seven ideas at a time and finds simplicity a huge mental relief. The typical employee likes predictability and consistency in his or her job—while still having an outlet for creative energy. The typical employee likes to be part of a winning team and, research shows, craves clarity about strategy and core values above all else.

We end with our top ten conclusions. Each runs as a recurring theme through the entire book, so you should recognize them all. They cut across several different topics—how the world is changing and what it means for strategy, the power of the Great Repeatable Models, the design principles of strategies built around repeatable models, and their benefits and, of course, their limitations.

The Top Ten Conclusions

1. *The nature of business strategy is changing fundamentally due to speed, turbulence, and complexity of markets.* Enduring strategy is becoming much more about deep capabilities and the ability to adapt than about detailed plans. We now inhabit a world where the ability to sense and react is more realistic to pursue than the ability to anticipate or predict all possibilities.

2. *Most management teams find that successful growth strategies drive them farther and farther from the front line and from the customer,* sowing seeds of slower reaction, reduced self-awareness, and a decreased ability to learn and improve. Indeed, a majority of people in the average company feel that they do not understand the strategy. The customer suffers, and is the first and most direct victim of the diseconomies of scale. Yet, few management teams think about this or recognize the

gap; it happens slowly and perniciously, like the story of heating a pan of water with a frog in it, one degree at a time, until it is too late and the frog has hardly noticed. Growth begets complexity, which is the silent killer of future growth. Repeatable models can help to control it. The natural tendency of organizations is to add complexity in the attempt to deal with complexity. Eventually, this is the opposite of what you should do. Excess complexity affects internal processes, external relationships with other companies, and, most of all, the customer.

3. *Repeatable models are the best way to capture your greatest successes and replicate them again and again.* Strategies built around repeatable models account for a large and increasing share of success stories in business. Repeatable models can create competitive advantage through a superior ability to drive learning, a greater ability to align the organization for faster implementation, and greater focus in innovation and adaptation.

4. *The Great Repeatable Models follow three design principles. Adherence to them explains nearly half of performance variations among businesses.* These are a well-differentiated core and an activity system to replicate it; a set of clear nonnegotiable principles to translate strategy through the organization to the front line; and systems to drive learning and adaptation.

5. *The strategic power of continuous improvement is enormously undervalued.* Yet, this is a major benefit of repeatable models (due to their transparency, information flow, and ability to compare).

Small differences in the ability to improve, compounded year after year, have proved to be decisive in many competitive battles, improving both performance for the customer and the ability to reinvest due to superior cost performance.

6. *The most effective strategies are those that are pulled up the organization from below versus those that are pushed down aggressively from above.* Nonnegotiables that translate strategy into a few key principles to guide behavior and decisions can help. They should be cocreated through layers of the organization and, eventually, find their way into the core processes and routines. Repeatable models have a big advantage here.

7. *Entropy is a hidden destroyer of value of repeatable models.* The leader must be the custodian of the three design principles of repeatable models, and make the appropriate trade-offs for that business between the freedom to choose and change on the one hand, and the requirement to stay within the framework of the model on the other.

8. *Most cases of stall-out or loss of strategic momentum are due to premature abandonment of the core model.* This can occur due to failure to see the core's full potential, to boredom or hubris, or simply to taking the core capabilities for granted. All are fundamentally human error. Less than one-third of cases were due to obsolescence of part of the core model or sudden, disruptive external shifts. Repeatable models increase self-awareness of the core. This makes full potential easier to see, creating more confidence that it is real.

9. *Nearly all emergency attempts at "radical strategic redefinitions" fail; repeatable models can help to prevent the need for this through earlier and more measured responses.* Radical plans to redefine a business under stress usually prove to be the result of slow or inadequate response, despite resources and plenty of time, to the need to adapt the model. When this happens, it is usually a by-product of past mistakes and delays. The ability to adapt is one of the most important competitive separators in more and more markets. Systems to learn and adapt should no longer be an add-on but an essential and nonnegotiable part of strategies in dynamic markets.

10. *The power of focus is constantly underestimated, or ignored, in a world of constant change. Above all, repeatable models are about how to combine maniacal focus with the need for constant adaptation.* This is the most common theme of the Great Repeatable Models and the ultimate challenge of their leaders.

It is just possible that Great Repeatable Model companies of the future will turn a triple play of advantages. They will be faster to the ball relative to competitors. They will be a better teammate for their ecosystem partners. And they will be a more motivating and rewarding place to work for their employees—perhaps the most important benefit of all.

They are simply better places in which to invest to build wealth or to build a career. Year after year after year.

Appendix 1

Research Methodology

Companies Researched

We studied a wide range of companies across industries, in both mature and emerging markets, to understand how the great repeatable business models work in practice. The overview below provides a list of the companies that were most influential for the theses of the book. Many of them are profiled in the main text.

We started by looking at several hundred companies that appeared in lists of successful companies (such as the *Fortune* 500), showed up in our own analyses of best-performing companies, or were suggested to us by our colleagues or clients. We then applied the following criteria for each of these companies in order to select the following list:

- Mature, proven business model, typically more than $1 billion in annual sales

- Outperforming its competitors and/or peers on key financial metrics for an extended period of time (at least a decade)—some of the companies in this list later stalled out after a long period of success; for those companies, we studied both the reasons for their success and the reasons for their subsequent decline

- Employing a clear repeatable model to grow

- A balance of industry, geography, and type of repeatable model across the entire list

TABLE A1-1

Company	Industry	Country	Sales ($B)	Remarks
AmBev	CP/retail	Brazil	14	
American Express	Financial services	United States	28	a
Amore Pacific	CP/retail	Korea	1.7	
Apple	Tech/media/telco	United States	65	a
ASML	Tech/media/telco	Netherlands	6	
Bain Capital	Private equity	United States	38c	
Berkshire Hathaway	Various	United States	136	
BHP Billiton	Industrial	Australia	53	
Cisco	Tech/media/telco	United States	40	
Danaher	Industrial	United States	13	a
DaVita	Health care	United States	6	a, b
Dell	Tech/media/telco	United States	52	b
Endemol	Tech/media/telco	Netherlands	2	
Enterprise	CP/retail	United States	13	
Express Scripts	Health care	United States	25	
FloraHolland	Retail	Netherlands	0.4	a
Gore	Industrial	United States	2.5	
Hankook Tire	Industrial	Korea	5	
Harley-Davidson	Industrial	United States	5	
Hilti	Industrial	Liechtenstein	4	

Huawei	Tech/media/telco	China	28	
IKEA	CP/retail	Sweden	30	
ITT	Industrial	United States	11	
Larsen & Toubro	Industrial	India	12	a
LEGO	CP/retail	Denmark	1.5	
Li & Fung	Industrial	Hong Kong	16	a
LVMH	CP/retail	France	27	
Medtronic	Health care	United States	16	
MSC	Industrial	United States	1.7	a
Nike	CP/retail	United States	21	a, b
Nine Dragons	Industrial	Hong Kong	3	
Nokia	Tech/media/telco	Finland	56	a, b
Novozymes	Industrial	Denmark	1.7	
Olam	Industrial	Singapore	8	a
P&G	CP/retail	United States	79	
Publix	CP/retail	United States	25	b
Reckitt Benckiser	CP/retail	United Kingdom	13	
Scania	Industrial	Sweden	11	
Sherwin-Williams	Industrial	United States	8	
Singapore Airlines	Airlines	Singapore	11	
Sodexo	CP/retail	France	21	
Starbucks	CP/retail	United States	11	
Tesco	CP/retail	United Kingdom	94	b
Tetra Pak	Industrial	Switzerland/Sweden	14	a
Toyota	Industrial	Japan	222	b
TSMC	Tech/media/telco	Taiwan	13	
Unilever	CP/retail	United Kingdom/Netherlands	59	a
UTC	Industrial	United States	54	
Vanguard	Financial services	United States	1,600[d]	a

(continued)

Company	Industry	Country	Sales ($B)	Remarks
Vodafone	Tech/media/telco	United Kingdom	71	a
Vopak	Industrial	Netherlands	1	

Note: CP = consumer products; tech/media/telco = technology, media, and telecommunications.
a. Authors conducted in-person interviews with executives.
b. Performed peer-to-peer comparison with less repeatable counterpart: DaVita vs. Gambro (preacquisition), Dell vs. Gateway, Nike vs. Reebok, Nokia vs. Motorola, Publix vs. A&P, Tesco vs. Sainsbury, and Toyota vs. GM.
c. Ten-year cumulative capital raised.
d. Assets under management.
Sources: Bain 200 Company Database of Repeatable Models; Capital IQ; Worldscope; Bain analysis.

In appendix 3, we have written a short synopsis of the story for each of the top twenty-five case examples used in the book.

Analyses of Best-Performing Companies

Group 1: Sustained Value Creators

The analysis of sustained value creators (SVCs) was published in the first edition of *Profit from the Core* in 2001.[1] Since then the analysis has been updated annually as part of the Bain Growth Project. SVCs are companies that satisfy the following criteria over a ten-year period:

- Growing both revenues and earnings at least 5.5 percent per year, after correction for inflation

- Earning cost of capital for shareholders

These criteria reflect the aspirations of most companies: in our internal sample of targets from strategic plans, more than 90 percent of companies had aimed at growth well in excess of these levels. In contrast, our analyses of more than five thousand companies in twelve major developed and emerging economies have shown that only about one in ten companies actually achieves these growth levels, even in the best of economic times.[2]

In researching this book, we used the analysis of SVCs in two ways:

- For the selection of case studies that we profiled

- For a comparison of repeatable models in a sample of twenty-six SVCs with twenty-six non-SVCs in the same sector, proving that the SVCs were more repeatable, in a statistically significant way

Group 2: Double SVCs

We also looked at the elite group of companies that achieved SVC levels of performance over the two consecutive decades between 1988 and 2008. Only twenty-three companies made it to the final version of this list.

Group 3: Rocket Ships

The other elite group that emerged from our analyses of our company database is the fastest-growing companies we call "rocket ships." They met the following criteria:

- Growing from less than $1 billion to more than $10 billion between 1987 and 2007

- Earning at least 15 percent total shareholder return per year over that growth period

FIGURE A1-1

Excess return, 1998-2008

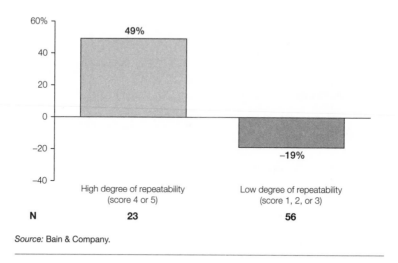

	High degree of repeatability (score 4 or 5)	Low degree of repeatability (score 1, 2, or 3)
N	23	56

Source: Bain & Company.

Two Hundred–Company Database

We developed a database of two hundred companies that included indicators of performance and the degree to which the company was perceived to be strong or weak in a range of practices like translating strategy into a few principles, having a clear and singular form of competitive differentiation, and being seen as best in its industry at responding and adapting to market shifts.

For the companies for which we had ten-year total shareholder returns available (N=79), we calculated the returns above the cost of capital over this period. We found a large and statistically significant (99 percent level) difference between high scorers and low scorers on the extent to which their core business model was repeatable (figure A1-1).

Furthermore, for the entire set of companies with all assessments available (N=200), we calculated the degree of adherence to each of the design principles as defined in the main text of

Average score on adherence to each of the design principles

	Company performance		
	Bottom 30%	Next 50%	Top 20%
DP1: repeatable differentiation	2.9	3.7	4.4
DP2: routines and nonnegotiables	2.8	3.3	4.0
DP3: feedback loops	2.1	2.6	3.5

Source: Bain 200 Company Database of Repeatable Models.

the book, by performance bucket of the company. For each of the design principles, we found clear and statistically significant (99.9 percent level) differences between the performance buckets on the adherence scores to the design principles.

The performance groups in the table (bottom 30 percent, next 50 percent, and top 20 percent) have been used throughout the book and are based on the performance assessed by the survey participants. For the companies with shareholder returns available (N=79), the assessed performance links in a statistically significant manner (99 percent level) to excess return (i.e., total shareholder return above the cost of capital), which gave us confidence that we could use the assessed performance as a good proxy for actual company performance.

EIU Survey

In March 2011, we surveyed 377 executives across geographies, industries, and company sizes (see figure A1-2 for the survey demographics), in conjunction with the Economist Intelligence Unit. We have used the results of this survey in three ways:

- To reconfirm the link between performance and the three design principles

FIGURE A1-2

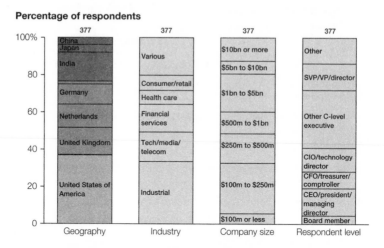

Percentage of respondents

Source: Bain/EIU "Repeatable Model" survey, March 2011 (n = 377).

- To add further data to the book about executives' views on the business environment, growth strategies, and repeatable models

- To develop an objective benchmarking set to diagnose other companies (see appendix 2)

Leadership Analysis

To show the extent to which leaders are able to sustain their leadership under turbulence, we selected ten turbulent industries, such as automotive, telecom, and banking. For each of the ten industries, we selected two businesses that in 2000 had a clear market leader. For each of those twenty companies, we assessed the extent to which they were still market leaders in 2010, with the following results:

- Six companies were still clear market leaders (examples: McDonald's in fast food and Goldman Sachs in investment banking)

- Seven companies faced significant challenges to their market leadership (examples: Nokia in mobile handsets and British Airways in European passenger air transport)

- Seven companies were clearly overtaken by one or more competitors (examples: Hertz in U.S. car rental [by Enterprise] and AltaVista in Web search [by Google])

Stall-Out Analysis

To understand the key drivers of stall-out performance, and whether it was avoidable, we looked at forty companies that "stalled." As a starting point, we took the key lists of stall-outs from the following sources:

- Jim Collins, *How the Mighty Fall*

- Gary Hamel and C. K. Prahalad, *Competing for the Future*

- Matthew Olson and Derek van Bever, *Stall Points*

- The previous books of the authors of this work, *Profit from the Core, Beyond the Core,* and *Unstoppable*

We included only stall-outs after 1980 that left a clear mark in share price performance (for listed companies) and financial performance (revenue growth and profitability), to arrive at our list of forty. We classified the reasons for stall-outs in three groups:

1. *Losing focus on the core.* Companies in this group stalled, according to external observers, because of a lack of focus in their strategy, leading to a distraction from a once successful core business. Close to two-thirds of companies fell into this group, including Vivendi, Reebok, and Citigroup.

2. *Failure to adapt.* Companies in this group failed to adapt their core to changes in technology, customer preferences, and/or other key trends. In our sample, about 30 percent were in this group, such as Blockbuster, Xerox, and Digital Equipment Corporation (DEC).

3. *Other.* Companies in this group couldn't be classified into one of the other two buckets. The two companies from our sample in this category were airlines that couldn't compete effectively after the deregulation of the U.S. airline industry.

Furthermore, we classified the performance after the stall-out period:

- *Recovered.* Clear recovery in revenues, profitability, and shareholder value. ~15 percent of total sample; examples: Apple and American Express.

- *Driven into marginality.* No recovery of destroyed shareholder value or a marginal role versus the industry-leading position before the stall-out. ~20–25 percent of total sample; examples: Kodak and Bausch & Lomb.

- *Acquired/split.* Acquired, split, or otherwise dissolved through M&A activity. ~35 percent of total sample; examples: Motorola and Reebok.

- *Bankrupt.* Company went into bankruptcy or bankruptcy protection, with (almost) complete loss of shareholder value. ~20-25 percent of total sample; examples: A&P and Blockbuster.

- *Not yet clear.* The level of recovery in terms of financials, shareholder value, and competitive position was inconclusive as of this writing. ~5 percent of total sample; examples: HP and Starbucks.

Appendix 2

How Repeatable Are You?

You can use this diagnostic to assess your repeatability against the bottom, average, and top performers in our database. The diagnostic will clearly show on which dimensions specifically you are doing well or falling behind other companies. The diagnostic is a simplified version of the strategy diagnostic that Bain & Company uses with its clients. Go to www.repeat ability.com/diagnostic to access the interactive version of the diagnostic.

To do the diagnostic, please indicate to what extent you (and your colleagues) agree with each of the statements, and apply the following scoring scale:

Strongly agree:	+50
Agree more than disagree:	+25
Don't agree, don't disagree:	0
Disagree more than agree:	−25
Strongly disagree:	−50

For negatively formulated statements (marked *negative*), please invert the scoring scale (i.e., add points if you disagree and subtract points if you agree). Then add all points by each group of four questions to determine your score for each design principle. You can benchmark yourself against the 350-plus executives we surveyed in conjunction with the Economist Intelligence Unit, split by their level of performance in comparison with competitors.

TABLE A2-1

Repeatable model diagnostic

Design principle	Question	Your score
1: A well-differentiated core	1a. We have strong consensus in our management team around a clear and simple strategy.	_____
	1b. Our strategy is built around a few core capabilities that are highly differentiated versus competitors' and well understood in our organization.	_____
	1c. Our strategy is built around a repeatable model that we constantly apply with a high success rate to new markets and segments.	_____
	1d. We don't make sharp enough investment decisions, spreading our resources too thin across too many initiatives.	_____ (negative)
	Total	_____
	Benchmarks by performance group	Top: 79 Average: 46 Bottom: −13

2: Clear nonnegotiables

2a. Our front line understands our strategy and is fully in line with top management. _____

2b. The essence of our strategy has been translated into a few (5–10) well-defined principles that drive consistent behaviors and decisions across the organization. _____

2c. We are able to replicate successes and best practices from one part of our organization to other parts (i.e., geographies, segments, product lines, etc.). _____

2d. We have too many management layers. _____ (negative)

Total _____

Benchmarks by performance group   Top: 79
Average: 49
Bottom: –5

3: Closed-loop learning

I. Continuous improvement

3a. We are the best in our industry at capturing learning and driving continuous improvement in all key functions. This is a competitive advantage. _____

3b. Our senior managers and executives spend enough time with key customers to understand their most important needs and key trends affecting them. _____

3c. There is too much variation in practices across our company. This reduces our ability to learn and to execute fast enough. _____ (negative)

3d. We have too many or too complex IT systems. _____ (negative)

Total (part I) _____

(continued)

Design principle	Question	Your score
3: Closed-loop learning (cont.)	**II. Adaptive strategy**	
	3e. We are good at making decisions and executing them fast.	_____
	3f. We innovate and experiment in the field a lot. This drives our learning and is a competitive advantage.	_____
	3g. We do not highlight and confront the biggest challenges to our business model fast enough.	_____ (negative)
	3h. We are too busy fighting the daily battle to step back.	_____ (negative)
	Total (part II)	_____
	Average of I and II	_____
	Benchmarks by performance group	Top: 70 Average: 28 Bottom: –32

Appendix 3

Summary of
Top Thirty Case Studies

Below we have summarized the thirty most important case examples we have used in this book. They are listed in alphabetical order.

AB Inbev is today the combination of Ambev, the leading beer company in South America; Interbrew, one of the leaders in Europe; and, recently, Anheuser-Busch, the leader in North America. It is now the largest beer company in the world, with 2010 revenues of $36 billion. Central to the success of AB Inbev is its repeatable model for managing costs, operations, and assets, which traces much of its origin to the Brazilian Ambev. Ambev reports separate results, not distorted by the continuous string of combinations driving the parent company, and has shown a return to shareholders of 29 percent during the past ten years.

American Express's repeatable model for charge cards and payment systems traces back to 1850. During the fifteen years up to the 2008 financial crisis, American Express increased profits by ten times and achieved 17 percent annual return to shareholders, while gaining considerable market share in its core card business and remaining highly profitable throughout the 2008–2009 financial crisis. CEO Ken Chenault has referred to American Express as "a company of repeatable models."[1]

Since the launch of the first iPod in 2001, *Apple* has driven its strategy through a series of repeatable models defined by the sequence of its products (iPod, iPad, iPod touch, MacBook Air, iPhone, Apple TV), by the sequence of content on iTunes (music, video, TV, books, etc.), and through its geographic expansion. During the ten years from 2001 to 2010, Apple grew its profits from a loss to $18 billion in operating income and to a market value of over $250 billion, making it the most valuable technology company in the world.

ASML is the world market leader in manufacturing lithography equipment that allows its customers, such as Intel, Samsung, and TSMC, to make ever-smaller, faster, and more efficient electronic chips for computers, tablets, and smart phones. ASML was founded in 1984, and used to be a small player in the lithography space, with Japanese giants Nikon and Canon as its main competitors. By consistently focusing on developing the best lithography equipment and investing throughout the economic cycle, it was able to become market leader in 2002. Since then ASML has consolidated its leadership position, and now effectively is the only player in the top segment of the market.

Berkshire Hathaway is the investment vehicle of multibillionaire Warren Buffett. The company aims to "maximize Berkshire's average annual rate of gain in intrinsic business value on a per-share basis," following a short set of investment principles, buying underperforming businesses, improving them, and holding them for the long term."[2] Over the past two decades, Berkshire has returned 16 percent per year to its shareholders.

BHP Billiton is the world's largest mining company. In 2001 the Australian Broken Hill Proprietary (BHP) and the South African Billiton merged to become the company that would turn out to be the most successful player in the mining industry. BHP Billiton acquires strong "tier 1" mines when they are underpriced due to the economic cycle. Its diversified portfolio, along with a strong, relatively stable cash flow then enables it to invest in improving the mining operations. Moreover, BHP Billiton has proved to be very successful in reducing the enormous complexity of running a $53 billion corporation with more than one hundred operations in twenty-five countries, producing a dozen different commodities. For instance, it has reduced the nine thousand different management authorities that it identified throughout the company to just thirty. In the eight years since the merger, BHP Billiton has grown revenues at 15 percent per year and operating income at 29 percent while generating an annual total shareholder return of 22 percent.

Danaher has been the best-performing multicore company ("conglomerate") in the world over the past twenty years. The company has been built up by a series of acquisitions—about eighty-five companies during the past ten years, with the parent corporation each time applying the Danaher Business System (its repeatable model) to increase consistently the margins of the acquired companies by up to ten points. Today, the Danaher Business System has become the way the company manages its business and the way the center adds value. In 2010 Danaher grew to a $13 billion company with $1.8 billion of earnings. An investor who invested $100 in Danaher in 1989 would have about $10,000 now for that investment; over the past twenty years, Danaher has returned an average of 24 percent per year to shareholders.

DaVita's repeatable model is the development and management of centers for the treatment of renal failure patients. In 1999, the company was in serious trouble, with revenues of $1.4 billion, losses of $67 million, a government investigation, 40 percent employee turnover, and stock price collapse. Today, DaVita has attained sustained value creator status for ten years, growing to $6.4 billion in revenue in 2010, increasing its market share from 12 percent to 29 percent, and driving its stock price from below $2 per share in 2000 to more than $70 per share at the end of 2010. The turnaround of DaVita is a classic example of the power of all three of our design principles to turn around a business and create value.

Enterprise Rent-A-Car runs the largest private fleet of vehicles in the world, of more than a million cars. The company began in 1957 to provide what it calls "replacement" rentals to people whose vehicles were disabled or under repair. Today, Enterprise has achieved more than 70 percent market share in this specialized rental niche, using one of the best examples of a repeatable model adhering to our three design principles that we have found. In recent years, Enterprise has used its cash flow to purchase the Alamo and National car rental businesses, expanding into adjacencies of leisure and business airport travel, where it is now applying the elements of its repeatable model.

Hankook Tire has been one of the fastest-growing tire companies in the world during the past decade. Its repeatable model is centered on its ability to build and manage low-cost tire plants. The company started as a low-cost and lower-quality Korean tire company, but through its model of continuous improvement has maintained its cost levels while achieving world-class quality levels. From 2001 to the end of the decade, Hankook increased its stock price by ten times and became a leader in the fastest-growing Asian markets, such as China and Korea.

Hilti is a Liechtenstein-based company in the business of designing and distributing tools and supplies for the construction industry. Its repeatable model is built around a direct-to-customer distribution system (nearly all of the market is indirect) and its methods of working closely with the customer to design tools with superior functionality—driving a price premium of more than 20 percent in many of its core product lines, like drilling systems. Hilti has a consistent 6 percent growth rate over fifty years and a track record of continuous profitability.

In less than a decade, *Huawei* has grown from a cheap, "me too" electronics manufacturer that no Western company had heard of, into one of the world's leading and most innovative telecom and network equipment suppliers. Huawei is viewed today by many traditional telecom equipment vendors as their primary competitive threat of the future. Its largely employee-owned organization is focused on fast cycle times and a short distance between management and the front line. Huawei's installation times are dramatically shorter than for incumbents, with similar or better product quality and 20–30 percent lower prices. In 2002 Huawei's revenues were $2.1 billion in size; by 2010 they reached $27 billion, a more than tenfold increase in eight years—with industry-leading (14 percent) profit margins.

IKEA is the most successful furniture manufacturer and retailer in the world. Since its founding in 1943, IKEA has consistently refined and improved its repeatable model. The IKEA model contains many differentiated elements, from its store layout to its flat packaging of all furniture for customer assembly to the way it designs and sources furniture to tiered price points. IKEA's core market is Europe, where it is nearly ten times as large as its nearest competitor. Over the past twenty-five years, IKEA has grown by 13 percent per year in a market that grows

5 percent per year. IKEA's operating margins are above 15 percent, more than double the industry average profit level.

Larsen & Toubro (L&T) is the largest infrastructure construction organization in India, with operations extending far
beyond the Indian subcontinent. The company traces its origin
to 1938, with the wonderful signature phrase "we make things
that make India proud." Since A. M. Naik became CEO in 1999,
L&T has grown its revenues at 22 percent, to $12 billion, and its
profits at a 45 percent annual rate, to $1 billion. Central to this
success were a period of shrinking to its construction core in
order to grow and the application of a repeatable approach to
project-based large-scale construction.

Since 1955, *LEGO* has focused on perfecting and extending
its "LEGO system of play" with its signature product, familiar
interlocking plastic blocks. The LEGO system itself is a metaphor for the repeatability of its business model, which has
resulted in more than sixty LEGO blocks for every person on
earth and its designation as "toy of the century." In an aspiration
to become "the strongest brand to families with children"[3] during the 1990s, LEGO departed from its core repeatable model,
to its peril, declining to a level of losses of 28 percent of revenues
in 2004, having destroyed an average of €300,000 per day for
more than ten years. Jørgen Vig Knudstorp became CEO of the
company in 2004 and has engineered a return to the repeatable
model of the past, and its renewal, driving profitability up to 25
percent of revenues in 2009. Even during the economic down-
turn, the company's repeatable model generated continuous
market share gains and earnings growth of 55 percent per year.

Li & Fung is the most successful manager of manufacturing
supply chains running from Asia (especially China) to Europe
and North America. The company traces its origins to an export

company in 1906 and its current strategy to a complete redefinition of its business model by the brothers William and Victor Fung during the 1980s. From 1999 to 2009, Li & Fung achieved 20 percent annual revenue growth, 20 percent profit growth, and 25 percent total return to shareholders per year. Fueling its growth is a highly repeatable business model organized around individual customers for the management of their complete supply chain—sometimes all the way to the door of the retail store.

Louis Vuitton is one of the most aspirational global brands—customers around the world are willing to pay $1,000 or more to own one of the timeless handbags with the famous LV logo. Its repeatable model consists of showcasing a mix of classic and fashionable design through its own retail locations, with superior quality, customization, and service—and no discounts, ever. Over the past decade, the brand grew by 10 percent annually (market growth was 3 percent), with operating profit margins of more than 40 percent—beating its competitors by at least 10 to 20 percentage points.

MSC is the leading distributor in the United States of supplies for the metalworking industry. The company traces its origins to Sid Tool company, a local distributor in Lower Manhattan in 1941. In 1994 the management team recognized that they had the elements of a business with leadership economics and a repeatable model to expand nationally. In a low-growth market, MSC grew from $194 million to $1.7 billion by 2010, a rate of 16 percent per year.

NIKE is the world's leading supplier of athletic shoes and equipment. The company traces its origin to the original "Waffle Trainer," which started a revolution in running shoe design. The company was founded in 1964 by Phil Knight, who remains chairman today. NIKE is one of the best examples we have seen of a repeatable model, honed over a long period of time, and focused on identifying, entering, and increasing the industry profit pool in one segment of sports after another, from tennis to cycling to football. Over a twenty-five-year period, NIKE increased sales and earnings more than twenty times, and shareholder investments more than one hundred times—a total 20 percent annual shareholder return during this period.

Olam began in 1989 with a project to bring cashews from Nigeria to the food producers of Europe. Over time, the management team, led by CEO Sunny Verghese, developed a repeatable model to manage risk and supply chains for agricultural products from developing economies to food producers. We found that Olam is one of the best examples in the world of our three design principles of Great Repeatable Models from start-up to maturity. Olam has experienced more than 25 percent annual growth rates in earnings and profits since 2001. It has now extended its repeatable model to more than sixty countries, fourteen products, and multiple new processing steps in the supply chains, achieving a revenue level in 2010 of just over $8 billion. Since its IPO in 2005, the share price has more than tripled despite a difficult industry cycle.

Procter & Gamble is one of the most enduring and iconic consumer products companies, with products spanning from Tide detergent to Gillette shavers. From 1996 through 2001, earnings were flat and the company seemed to have stalled out. A. G. Lafley, a longtime P&G loyalist, took over as CEO, with a mission to rejuvenate and strengthen the company's famous repeatable model for managing brand businesses, focus the portfolio, and develop new products. The strategy worked, leading to an 18 percent annual increase in profits from $5.9 billion to $17.9 billion EBIT. Fifteen of P&G's twenty-one core brands are leaders in their category today. We used this example in the book to illustrate the power of renewing your repeatable model of the past.

Reckitt Benckiser is formally based in the United Kingdom but describes itself as a "global" FMCG company. The company was created from the merger between British Reckitt & Colman and Dutch Benckiser in 1999. Since then it has grown revenues at 10 percent annually and profits at 31 percent, and created an annual shareholder return of 17 percent—far outperforming its larger rivals, such as P&G, Unilever, and Colgate-Palmolive. It has done so by employing a strategy that is focused on building a few extremely strong "power brands" (e.g., Calgon, Clearasil, and Finish) and investing heavily in the innovation and marketing of these brands—even throughout the financial crisis. In 2006 the CEO stated that he intended "to do plenty more of the same, . . . repeating our strategy for delivering profitable growth. We believe that the simplicity and clarity of our strategy helps us with the execution as our strategy is so well understood throughout the Company."[4]

Scania is the leading manufacturer of trucks for the European market, based in Södertälje, Sweden. In the fifteen years up to the financial crisis, it grew revenues fivefold to SEK 89B (about $13 billion). Scania has realized this growth by doubling down on its core European heavy truck market, divesting its aviation business, and consciously leaving alone the very different U.S. market. It continuously expanded its core customer base in Western Europe, as well as the services it offered to those customers, such as financing, parts logistics, and fleet management. Scania then replicated this model into the high-growth Eastern European countries and other emerging markets. Its share price has multiplied threefold between 2000 and 2010, and throughout the crisis Scania has remained profitable for every single quarter, while financials in Q3 of 2010 were back again at precrisis levels.

Singapore Airlines successfully pursued a strategy of a highly differentiated customer service combined with low-cost operations. It has won the World's Best Airline award from *Condé Nast Traveler* an astonishing twenty-two of twenty-three times, with costs per available seat kilometer lower than those of most other Asian airlines and just a third of the level of some of the traditional European airlines. In an industry that is notorious for its value destruction, Singapore Airlines has been profitable every single year since its founding in 1972, and between 1995 and 2009 it realized a 9 percent annual total shareholder return.

France-based *Sodexo* is one of the leading food service providers globally. It started in 1966, serving good-quality food to French company restaurants, schools, and hospitals. Since then, it has continuously improved and replicated its model into new services (e.g., maintenance), client segments (e.g., remote sites), and geographies (e.g., Belgium, the United Kingdom, and the United States). Throughout its expansion, Sodexo has maintained a very strong frontline focus, with about 95 percent of its employees working on its sites. Sodexo has an industry-leading client retention rate of 94.2 percent, and has realized an after-inflation revenue and profit growth of more than 10 percent per year over the past twenty years.

Tesco is the leading grocery chain in the United Kingdom. The company revolutionized its industry during the 1990s (despite the fact it was founded in 1919) by bringing to the U.K. market a large-volume, low-cost, high-service concept that included such innovations as customer discounts if the wait time at checkout is more than a few minutes. Over the past twenty-five years, Tesco has achieved 13 percent annual revenue growth, 16 percent profit growth, and an average of 16 percent shareholder return per year. Tesco's repeatable model extends from its store model and supply chain management to the way it enters new categories, from petrol to pharmacy. In 2010 Tesco attained a scale of more than $90 billion and a U.K. market share of more than 30 percent.

Tetra Pak is a Swedish company whose repeatable model is built around its familiar laminated brick packs for foods and beverages. This private business traces its origins to its founding by Ruben Rausing in Lund, Sweden, in 1951. Tetra Pak is the overwhelming leader in this form of packaging and has experienced continuous growth and profitability for more than thirty-five years, now achieving a level of 158 billion packs sold per year and revenues of about $14 billion. The Tetra Pak system is highly repeatable, from its laminated materials to its machine configurations to its country organizations. Central to its strength as a company are core principles and beliefs put in place by the founder and nurtured and refined through successive generations of managers.

Toyota, the Japanese automobile company, is the father of many repeatable models in the world of heavy manufacturing. The Toyota system has been constantly studied, and copied, but never equaled. Toyota's repeatable approach to cell manufacturing and continuous improvement has brought it from a low-cost, low-quality, niche producer in the 1970s to a global top-3 leader today. An example of the power of the Toyota model is the way in which it displaced General Motors in the U.S. market, from 3 percent market share in 1980 to 17 percent in 2010.

During the past few years, Toyota encountered a series of crises around potential defects. Subsequent investigation has largely exonerated Toyota.

United Technologies Corporation (UTC) with $54 billion in 2010 revenues, has been one of the five best-performing multibusiness conglomerates in the world over the past fifteen years, with product lines running from Sikorsky helicopters to Carrier air-conditioning—all heavily engineered, industrial, global products. Central to the success of UTC is its corporate repeatable model, called Achieving Competitive Excellence (ACE). ACE is an operating model that defines a consistent management system across all of UTC's businesses, from plant floor management to customer relationship management. Businesses are graded according to their performance along a consistent set of ACE dimensions, and ACE is central to how the company defines how it adds value to its portfolio companies. UTC is an example of how a diverse company can still benefit from some of the principles of repeatable models. From 1994 to 2009, UTC achieved annual shareholder returns of 17 percent.

Vanguard was founded by John Bogle in 1974 as an investment company built around a set of investment principles that have remained at its core since then. Central to the Vanguard repeatable model is the idea that most investors cannot beat the market, that index funds are often the best way to invest, that loyal customers dominate all else, and that the company would not pay for distribution by others. Today, Vanguard is the world's largest mutual fund company, with $1.6 trillion under management. During the financial crisis from 2008 to 2009, Vanguard captured 45 percent of all the available investment funds in the United States. CEO Bill McNabb said to us that "Vanguard is at its core a repeatable model."

Appendix 4

Lexicon of Key Terms

Below we have listed the key terms that we use throughout the book. We only explain terms that aren't broadly used in general business language. For all terms, we refer for further explanation to chapters in this book, one of our earlier books, or other books or articles. Terms in the explanations that appear in *italics* are further explained in separate lemmas.

TABLE A4-1

Activity system	The combination of the *core sources of differentiation* and their key supporting activities, which jointly encompass the competitive advantage of a company. See chapter 2 of this book.
Adjacency	A business within a company that is not part of its *core*, but is economically related to it through cost, customer, channel, competitor, or capability sharing. See *Beyond the Core*.
Closed-loop learning	A system to continuously improve and adapt to changing market conditions by rapidly collecting the relevant data and immediately acting on it, in analogy to the military *OODA loop*. See chapter 4 of this book.
Continuous improvement	An approach to creating long-term value by incrementally improving the key business processes of the *repeatable model* to, e.g., reduce cost or create more loyal customers. Contrasts with one-off reorganizations. See chapter 4 of this book.

(continued)

Core

The most successful business(es) in a company (*core markets*) as well as the drivers of success in it/them (*core differentiation*). A strong core is the source of *leadership economics*. See *Profit from the Core*.

Core differentiation

Also, *core sources of differentiation*. The key five to seven capabilities and assets that drive the successes of a company. They could be tangible (e.g., having the best cable network) or intangible (e.g., having the lowest-cost production systems or the best due diligence capabilities). See chapter 2 of this book.

Core market(s)

The intersection of products, customers, channels, geographies, and value chain activities in which a company achieves its highest levels of success, in terms of financial returns, customer loyalty, and competitive outperformance. See *Profit from the Core*.

Design principles

The three principles that define the most successful repeatable models studied in this book: a clear *core differentiation*, simple *nonnegotiables*, and *closed-loop feedback* to adapt. See chapters 2, 3, and 4 of this book.

Focus-expand-redefine (FER) cycle

The growth cycle most businesses go through: new businesses start with focusing on a core; once that is at full potential, they expand the core into adjacencies; and when the core differentiation runs out, they redefine into a new core, when the cycle starts again. The cycle speed can vary widely among industries. See *Profit from the Core*.

Great Repeatable Model

The way a company replicates its biggest successes again and again, continuously improving them while adapting to new markets and to the changing business landscape. The model adheres to the three *design principles*. See chapter 1 of this book.

Hidden asset

A small part of a company's differentiation, which can serve to build a new core once the key parts of the old core differentiation run out (in the *redefine* phase of *FER*). See *Unstoppable*.

Leadership economics

The reinforcing cycle of market leaders in a specific defensible business who are in principle able to command higher returns (supposing proper business definition and strong execution), which they can reinvest again to further build out their leadership. See *Profit from the Core*.

Net Promoter® score (NPS®)	A measure of customer loyalty, calculated by taking the percentage of customers that are promoters minus the percentage of detractors. See Reichheld, *The ultimate Question 2.0.*
Nonnegotiable	A companywide principle that is a critical pillar of a company's *core differentiation*, and which everybody should adhere to. Exceptions are rare, need to be escalated to executives, and are often due to a conflict or trade-off with other nonnegotiables. See chapter 3 of this book.
OODA loop	A continuous decision cycle originally developed by John Boyd for military combat operational processes, which demonstrate often rapidly changing conditions demanding fast, externally oriented decisions. It is increasingly applicable for business strategy too. OODA stands for observe, orient, decide, and act. See chapter 4 of this book.
Profit pool	The total profits earned at all points along an industry's value chain. This is an important tool to map turbulent industries, particularly if they have "choke points"—i.e., activities in the value chain that can command disproportionate returns. See Gadiesh et al., *How to Map Your Industry's Profit Pool.*
RAPID®[1]	A tool to map decision processes. Each letter corresponds to a role that a person or committee has in reaching a decision: R = recommend; A = agree; P = perform; I = input; D = decide. See Blenko et al., *Decide & Deliver.*
Repeatable model	See *Great Repeatable Model.*
Routine	A successful part of the daily/weekly/monthly activities that has been replicated throughout a company. Examples would be IKEA's standard process for designing furniture to a price point, Danaher's standard due diligence process, or Enterprise's branch managers calling back a customer who wasn't "completely satisfied." See chapter 3 of this book.
Sustained value creator (SVC)	A company that has achieved sustainable growth over a ten-year period, defined as 5.5% after-inflation CAGR in both sales and earnings, while earning the cost of capital to shareholders. These targets reflect the aspirations of more than 90% of companies, while only about 10% achieve them. Ninety-five percent of SVCs have one or multiple strong *core(s)* with *leadership economics*. See *Profit from the Core.*

---

[1] RAPID® is a registered trademark of Bain & Company Inc.

Notes

Chapter 1

1. Survey of 377 executives in North America, Western Europe, and Asia conducted by the Economist Intelligence Unit (EIU) on behalf of Bain, March 2011.

2. Chris Zook, *Profit from the Core: A Return to Growth in Turbulent Times,* with James Allen (Boston: Harvard Business Press, 2010).

3. Chris Zook, *Beyond the Core: Expand Your Market Without Abandoning Your Roots* (Boston: Harvard Business School Press, 2004).

4. Chris Zook, *Unstoppable: Finding Hidden Assets to Renew the Core and Fuel Profitable Growth* (Boston: Harvard Business School Press, 2007).

5. This topic is further explored in Ramon Casadesus Masanell and Joan E. Ricart, "How to Design a Winning Business Model," *Harvard Business Review,* January–February 2011.

6. Hermann Simon, *Hidden Champions of the 21st Century: Success Strategies of Unknown World Market Leaders* (New York: Springer, 2009).

7. The *Economist* redaction, "The Future of the Pencil," *Economist,* September 16, 2010.

8. Data from our two hundred–company database, March 2010, and the Bain/Economist Intelligence Unit survey, March 2011.

9. Clayton M. Christensen, *The Innovator's Dilemma: When New Technologies Cause Great Firms to Fail* (Boston: Harvard Business School Press, 1997).

10. Bain/EIU survey, March 2011.

11. Bill McNabb, interview by Chris Zook, Malvern, PA, November 11, 2009.

12. Daniel Michaels, "O'Leary Pilots Ryanair into Lead with 'Mad' Ideas for Cost Cuts," *Wall Street Journal,* December 9, 2009.

13. Anna Teo, "SIA's Success Secret Is a Tough Balancing Act," *Business Times,* July 29, 2010.

14. Nichola Groom, "Schultz Back as Starbucks CEO; US Expansion Slowed," *Reuters News*, January 7, 2008.

15. Kevin J. O'Brien, "Nokia's Success Bred Its Weakness; Stifling Bureaucracy Led to Lack of Action on Early Smartphone Innovation," *International Herald Tribune*, September 27, 2010.

16. Details can be found in Zook, *Unstoppable*.

17. Christensen, *The Innovator's Dilemma*.

Chapter 2

1. James Allen et al., *Closing the Delivery Gap: How to Achieve True Customer-Led Growth* (Boston: Bain & Company, 2005).

2. Confirmation bias has been widely described in the academic literature—e.g., Raymond S. Nickerson, "Confirmation Bias: A Ubiquitous Phenomenon in Many Guises," *Review of General Psychology* 2, no. 2, 175-220 (1998); and Barbara Koslowski and Mariano Maqueda, "What Is Confirmation Bias and When Do People Actually Have It?" *Merrill-Palmer Quarterly: Journal of Developmental Psychology*, Vol. 39(1), 104–130 (January 1993).

3. Michael E. Porter, "What Is Strategy?" *Harvard Business Review*, November–December 1996.

4. Sunny Verghese, telephone interview by Chris Zook, April 11, 2010.

5. Ibid.

6. Chris Zook, *Beyond the Core: Expand Your Market Without Abandoning Your Roots* (Boston: Harvard Business School Press, 2004).

7. *Kaizen* is Japanese for "improvement" or "change for the better," and is a critical component of most lean manufacturing systems, including the Danaher Business System.

8. We define *relative share* as the market share relative to the closest competitor, i.e., if you have 4× relative share, you are four times as large as your biggest competitor.

9. Larry Culp, interview by Chris Zook, Washington, DC, November 16, 2009.

10. Ibid.

11. Bain Learning Curve Study, July 2007, updated version of the study in the book by David Harding and Sam Rovit, *Mastering the Merger: Four Critical Decisions That Make or Break the Deal* (Boston: Harvard Business School Press, 2004).

12. Ibid.

13. Chris Zook, *Profit from the Core: A Return to Growth in Turbulent Times*, with James Allen (Boston: Harvard Business Press, 2010).

14. Jørgen Vig Knudstorp, telephone interview by Chris Zook, February 8, 2010.

15. Ibid.

16. Zook, *Beyond the Core*.

Chapter 3

1. Peter Miller, "Swarm Theory," *National Geographic*, July 2007.

2. A quick search of the Internet turns up a lot of debate on this topic, along with the observation that ants comprise many individual species while humans are only one (so it isn't really a fair comparison). Whatever the specifics, there is no doubt that ants as a group are remarkably successful.

3. Jeffrey K. Liker, *The Toyota Way* (New York: McGraw-Hill, 2004).

4. Dr. Newton Howard, *Evolution of Commander's Intent in the United States Military* (Washington, DC: Center for Advanced Defense Studies, 2007).

5. Michael Mulherin, "A Bridge Too Far? The Lost Art of Commander's Intent," *Infantry Magazine*, July 2009.

6. Bain & Company and the Economist Intelligence Unit, "Global Survey of Executive Perceptions and Intentions About Growth," October 2002.

7. James S. Kunen, "Enron's Vision (and Values) Thing," *New York Times*, January 19, 2002.

8. Liker, *The Toyota Way*.

9. Steven Spear and H. Kent Bowen, "Decoding the DNA of the Toyota Production System," *Harvard Business Review*, September–October 1999.

10. Ibid.

11. Bill McNabb, interview by Chris Zook, Malvern, PA, November 11, 2009.

12. Fred Reichheld, *The Ultimate Question: Driving Good Profits and True Growth* (Boston: Harvard Business School Press, 2006).

13. Tim Cook (COO, Apple Inc.), "Apple Inc. Q1 2009 Earnings Conference Call Final Transcript," Thomson StreetEvents, January 21, 2009.

14. See http://www.emu.dk/erhverv/merkantil_caseeksamen/doc/ikea/english_testament_2007.pdf.

15. Colin White, *Strategic Management* (New York: Palgrave Macmillan, 2004).

16. See Tony Schwartz et al., *Be Excellent at Anything: The Four Keys to Transforming the Way We Work and Live* (New York: Free Press reprint, 2011), previously published as *The Way We're Working Isn't Working*.

17. Peter F. Drucker, *The Essential Drucker* (Oxford: Elsevier Ltd., 2007).

18. Charlie Denson, telephone interview by Chris Zook, September 7, 2010.

19. Mitchell Jacobson, interview by Chris Zook, MSC headquarters, Long Island, New York, February 5, 2010.

20. Ibid.

21. Ibid.

22. David Sandler, "David's Delivery," *MSC Today*, October–November 2010.

23. Kent Thiry, telephone interview by Chris Zook, March 2, 2010.

24. Ibid.

25. Ibid.

Chapter 4

1. Bain/EIU survey, March 2011.

2. Irving L. Janis, *Groupthink: Psychological Studies of Policy Decisions and Fiascoes* (Boston: Houghton Mifflin, 1982).

3. Clayton M. Christensen, *The Innovator's Dilemma: When New Technologies Cause Great Firms to Fail* (Boston: Harvard Business School Press, 1997).

4. Geoff Colvin, *Talent Is Overrated: What Really Separates World-Class Performers from Everybody Else* (New York: Penguin Group, 2008).

5. Numbers are adjusted for stock splits 3: 1 and 2: 1.

6. Betsy Morris, "Steve Jobs Speaks Out," *Fortune*, March 7, 2008.

7. The presentation is among others displayed on http://www.danford.net/boyd/.

8. Fred Thompson, "Business Strategy and the Boyd Cycle," *Journal of Contingencies and Crisis Management* (June 1995).

9. Marcia W. Blenko, Michael C. Mankins, and Paul Rogers, *Decide & Deliver: 5 Steps to Breakthrough Performance in Your Organization* (Boston: Harvard Business Review Press, 2010).

10. Pius Baschera, interview by Chris Zook, Liechtenstein, October 5, 2009.

11. Rikki Chequer, "It's Good to Talk," *Commercial Motor*, October 25, 2007.

12. Kenneth Arrow, "The Economic Implications of Learning by Doing," *Review of Economic Studies* (June 1962).

13. Bruce Henderson, *Perspectives on Experience* (Boston: Boston Consulting Group, 1972).

14. Walter Kiechel III, *The Lords of Strategy: The Secret Intellectual History of the New Corporate World* (Boston: Harvard Business Press, 2010).

15. Scania Group, "Focus on Continuous Improvements," http://www.scania.com/scania-group/scania-in-brief/focus-on-continuous-improvements/.

16. Best Firms to Work For ranking of *Consulting* magazine, 2003–2011.

17. Louis V. Gerstner, *Who Says Elephants Can't Dance? Leading a Great Enterprise Through Dramatic Change* (New York: HarperCollins, 2003).

18. J. Bruce Harreld, Charles A. O'Reilly III, and Michael L. Tushman, "Dynamic Capabilities at IBM: Driving Strategy into Action," *California Management Review* (September 2007).

19. Ibid.

Chapter 5

1. Bain/EIU survey, March 2011.

2. Jim Collins, *Good to Great: Why Some Companies Make the Leap . . . and Others Don't* (New York: HarperCollins, 2001).

3. Carl E. Larson and Frank M. J. LaFasto, *Teamwork: What Must Go Right, What Can Go Wrong* (Newbury Park, CA: Sage Publications, 1989).

4. Jim Collins, *How the Mighty Fall: And Why Some Companies Never Give In* (New York: HarperCollins, 2009).

5. Chris Zook, *Profit from the Core: A Return to Growth in Turbulent Times*, with James Allen (Boston: Harvard Business Press, 2010).

6. Bruce Whitehall, "Julian Metcalfe, Passionate Perfectionist," *Food Service Europe*, February 14, 2007.

7. Isadore Sharp, Corporate Bios, Four Seasons, http://www.fourseasons.com/about_us/corporate_bios/isadore_sharp/.

8. Sydney Finkelstein and Eric Jackson, "Building Smart Leadership," *Breakout Performance*, December 14, 2006.

9. Jena McGregor, "Customer Service Champs," *BusinessWeek*, March 5, 2007.

10. Adam Bird, "McKinsey Conversations with Global Leaders: Paul Polman of Unilever," *McKinsey Quarterly*, October 2009.

11. Robert Wats, "The Good Brick Who Rebuilt Lego," *Telegraph*, December 17, 2006.

12. Kim Hjelmgaard, "Back from the Brick: How Lego Was Transformed," *MarketWatch*, December 23, 2009.

13. Paul Polman, interview by James Allen, London, December 10, 2010.

14. Peter F. Drucker, *Managing for Results: Economic Tasks and Risk-Taking Decisions* (New York: Harper & Row, 1964).

15. Sandy Ogg, interview by James Allen, London, May 22, 2009.

16. David Haines, interview by James Allen, London, March 9, 2011.

17. Paul Polman, "AGM Speech 2010," Unilever, May 12, 2010, http://www.unilever.com/mediacentre/speeches/2010/Paulpolmanagm-speech2010.aspx.

18. Gareth Penny, interview by James Allen, London, August 15, 2008.

19. Haines interview.

20. Andy Taylor, "Driving Smoothly"(video), *BusinessWeek*, January 23, 2008.

21. Ibid.

22. F. A. Martinez-Jerez, E. Corsi, and V. Dessain, "Gucci Group: Freedom Within the Framework," Field Case 109079 (Boston: Harvard Business School, 2011).

23. Ibid.

24. Polman interview.

25. Bain analysis on "Management Tools and Trends" survey data, 2009 (Darrell Rigby and Barbara Bilodeau, Bain & Company).

26. Nicky Oppenheimer, as witnessed by James Allen, London, 1999.

27. Ibid.

28. Chris Gent, interview by James Allen, London, March 22, 2011.

29. Ibid.

30. Ibid.

31. Ibid.

32. Christian Sandström, *When Digital Imaging Displaced Kodak Film* (Gothenburg, Sweden: Chalmers University of Technology, July 16, 2009).

33. Chris Zook, *Unstoppable: Finding Hidden Assets to Renew the Core and Fuel Profitable Growth* (Boston: Harvard Business School Press, 2007).

34. Thomas A. Stewart and Julia Kirby, "The Institutional Yes—An Interview with Jeff Bezos," *Harvard Business Review*, October 2007.

35. Ingvar Kamprad, "Testament of a Furniture Dealer," IKEA, 2007, http://www.emu.dk/erhverv/merkantil_caseeksamen/doc/ikea/english_testament_2007.pdf.

36. Gent interview.

37. Chris Zook, *Profit from the Core: A Return to Growth in Turbulent Times*, with James Allen (Boston: Harvard Business Press, 2010); and Bain analysis of forty stall-outs. Stall-outs were classified as avoidable in either of two cases: (1) the stall-out was due to a growth strategy that made the company grow too far from the core, or (2) the stall-out was due to a lack of

adaptation, while the company had clear hidden assets that would have allowed it to continue to compete successfully.

38. Claudia H. Deutsch, "At Kodak, Some Old Things Are New Again," *New York Times*, May 2, 2008.

39. Bain/EIU survey, March 2011.

Chapter 6

1. Alonzo L. McDonald, "Of Floating Factories and Mating Dinosaurs," *Harvard Business Review*, November–December 1986.

2. Carol Lewis, "The Customer Calls the Shots," *Times*, September 22, 2005.

3. Bain/EIU survey, March 2011.

4. Marco Iansiti and Roy Levien, "Strategy as Ecology," *Harvard Business Review*, March 2004; and James F. Moore, "Predators and Prey: A New Ecology of Competition," *Harvard Business Review*, May–June 1993.

Appendix 1

1. Chris Zook, *Profit from the Core: Growth Strategy in an Era of Turbulence*, with James Allen (Boston: Harvard Business School Press, 2001).

2. Please refer to Chris Zook, *Profit from the Core: A Return to Growth in Turbulent Times*, with James Allen (Boston: Harvard Business Press, 2010), for a more extensive discussion of sustained value creators.

Appendix 3

1. Ken Chenault, interview by Chris Zook, New York, May 24, 2005.
2. See BerkshireHathaway.com.
3. LEGO Annual Accounts presentation, 1999.
4. Reckitt Benckiser Annual Report, 2006.

Bibliography

Books

Beinhocker, Eric D. *The Origin of Wealth: The Radical Remaking of Economics and What It Means for Business and Society.* Boston: Harvard Business School Press, 2006.

Blenko, Marcia W., Michael C. Mankins, and Paul Rogers. *Decide & Deliver: 5 Steps to Breakthrough Performance in Your Organization.* Boston: Harvard Business Review Press, 2010.

Christakis, Nicholas A., and James H. Fowler. *Connected: The Surprising Power of Our Social Networks and How They Shape Our Lives.* New York: Little, Brown, 2009.

Christensen, Clayton M. *The Innovator's Dilemma: When New Technologies Cause Great Firms to Fail.* Boston: Harvard Business School Press, 1997.

Collins, James C., and Jerry I. Porras. *Built to Last: Successful Habits of Visionary Companies.* New York: HarperBusiness, 1997.

Collins, Jim. *Good to Great: Why Some Companies Make the Leap . . . and Others Don't.* New York: HarperCollins, 2001.

———. *How the Mighty Fall: And Why Some Companies Never Give In.* New York: HarperCollins, 2009.

Colvin, Geoff. *Talent Is Overrated.* New York: Penguin Press, 2008.

Drucker, Peter F. *The Essential Drucker.* Oxford: Elsevier Ltd., 2007.

Gerstner, Louis V. *Who Says Elephants Can't Dance? Leading a Great Enterprise Through Dramatic Change.* New York: HarperCollins, 2002.

Geus, Arie de. *The Living Company: Growth, Learning and Longevity in Business.* New York: Longview Publishing, 1997.

Gladwell, Malcolm. *The Tipping Point: How Little Things Can Make a Big Difference.* New York: Little, Brown, 2000.

Gottfredson, Mark, and Steve Schaubert. *The Breakthrough Imperative: How the Best Managers Get Outstanding Results.* New York: Collins, 2008.

Hamel, Gary, and C. K. Prahalad. *Competing for the Future.* Boston: Harvard Business School Press, 1994.

Harding, David, and Sam Rovit. *Mastering the Merger: Four Critical Decisions That Make or Break the Deal.* Boston: Harvard Business School Press, 2004.

Harvard Business Review. *HBR's Ten Must Reads on Leadership.* Boston: Harvard Business Press, 2011.

Henderson, Bruce. *Perspectives on Experience.* Boston: Boston Consulting Group, 1972.

Janis, Irving L. *Groupthink: Psychological Studies of Policy Decisions and Fiascoes.* Boston: Houghton-Mifflin, 1982.

Kiechel, Walter, III. *The Lords of Strategy: The Secret Intellectual History of the New Corporate World.* Boston: Harvard Business Press, 2010.

Liker, Jeffrey K. *The Toyota Way.* New York: McGraw-Hill, 2004.

Olson, Matthew S., and Derek van Bever. *Stall Points.* New Haven, CT: Yale University Press, 2008.

Porter, Michael E. *Competitive Strategy.* New York: Free Press, 1980.

Reichheld, Fred. *The Ultimate Question 2.0: How Net Promoter Companies Thrive in a Customer-Driven World.* Boston: Harvard Business School Press, 2011.

Reichheld, Frederick F. *Loyalty Rules! How Today's Leaders Build Lasting Relationships.* Boston: Harvard Business School Press, 2001.

Ridley, Matt. *Genome.* New York: HarperCollins, 2002.

Rother, Mike. *Toyota Kata.* New York: McGraw-Hill, 2010.

Simon, Hermann. *Hidden Champions of the 21st Century: Success Strategies of Unknown World Market Leaders.* New York: Springer, 2009.

Syed, Matthew. *Bounce: How Champions Are Made.* London: Fourth Estate, 2010.

Teece, David J. *Dynamic Capabilities and Strategic Management.* New York: Oxford University Press, 2009.

Watts, Duncan J. *Six Degrees: The Science of a Connected Age.* London: Vintage Press, 2004.

White, Colin. *Strategic Management.* New York: Palgrave Macmillan, 2004.

Zook, Chris. *Beyond the Core: Expand Your Market Without Abandoning Your Roots.* Boston: Harvard Business School Press, 2004.

———. *Profit from the Core: A Return to Growth in Turbulent Times.* With James Allen. Boston: Harvard Business Press, 2010.

———. *Unstoppable: Finding Hidden Assets to Renew the Core and Fuel Profitable Growth.* Boston: Harvard Business School Press, 2007.

Articles

Allen, James, Fred Reichheld, Barney Hamilton, and Rob Markey. *Closing the Delivery Gap: How to Achieve True Customer-Led Growth.* Boston: Bain & Company, 2005.

Arrow, Kenneth. "The Economic Implications of Learning by Doing." *Review of Economic Studies,* June 1962.

Bird, Adam. "McKinsey Conversations with Global Leaders: Paul Polman of Unilever." *McKinsey Quarterly,* October 2009.

Casadesus, Ramon, and Joan E. Ricart. "How to Design a Winning Business Model." *Harvard Business Review,* January–February 2011.

Chequer, Rikki. "It's Good to Talk." *Commercial Motor,* October 25, 2007.

Collins, Jim. "Level 5 Leadership: The Triumph of Humility and Fierce Resolve." *Harvard Business Review,* July–August 2005.

Deutsch, Claudia H. "At Kodak, Some Old Things Are New Again." *New York Times,* May 2, 2008.

Economist redaction. "The Future of the Pencil." *Economist,* September 18, 2010.

Faniel, Patrick. "Living Customer Focus from the Top Down: A Conversation with Geert van Kuyck, CMO, Royal Philips Electronics N.V." *Executive Issue,* January 2009.

Finkelstein, Sydney, and Eric Jackson. "Building Smart Leadership." *Breakout Performance,* December 14, 2006.

Goleman, Daniel, Richard Boyatzis, and Annie McKee. "Best of HBR on Emotionally Intelligent Leadership, 2nd Edition." *Harvard Business Review,* 2008.

Groom, Nichola. "Schultz Back as Starbucks CEO; US Expansion Slowed." *Reuters News,* January 7, 2008.

Harreld, J. Bruce, Charles A. O'Reilly III, and Michael L. Tushman. "Dynamic Capabilities at IBM: Driving Strategy into Action." *California Management Review,* September 2007.

Hjelmgaard, Kim. "Back from the Brick: How LEGO Was Transformed." *MarketWatch,* December 23, 2009.

Howard, Newton. "Evolution of Commander's Intent in the US Military." Washington, DC: Center for Advanced Defense Studies, 2005.

Iansiti, Marco, and Roy Levien. "Strategy as Ecology." *Harvard Business Review,* March 2004.

Koslowski, Barbara, and Mariano Maqueda. "What Is Confirmation Bias and When Do People Actually Have It?" *Journal of Developmental Psychology,* January 1993.

Kunen, James S. "Enron's Vision (and Values) Thing." *New York Times,* January 19, 2002.

Lewis, Carol. "The Customer Calls the Shots." *Times,* September 22, 2005.

Mankins, Michael C., and Richard Steele. "Turning Great Strategy into Great Performance." *Harvard Business Review,* July–August 2005.

Martinez-Jerez, F. A., E. Corsi, and V. Dessain. "Gucci Group: Freedom Within the Framework." Field Case 109079. Boston: Harvard Business School, 2011.

McDonald, Alonzo L. "Of Floating Factories and Mating Dinosaurs." *Harvard Business Review*, November–December 1986.

McGregor, Jena. "Customer Service Champs." *BusinessWeek*, March 5, 2007.

Michaels, Daniel. "O'Leary Pilots Ryanair into Lead with 'Mad' Ideas for Cost Cuts." *Wall Street Journal*, December 9, 2009.

Miller, Peter. "Swarm Theory." *National Geographic*, July 2007.

Moore, James F. "Predators and Prey: A New Ecology of Competition." *Harvard Business Review*, May–June 1993.

Morris, Betsy. "Steve Jobs Speaks Out." *Fortune*, March 7, 2008.

Mulherin, Michael. "A Bridge Too Far? The Lost Art of Commander's Intent." *Infantry Magazine*, July 2009.

Nickerson, Raymond S. "Confirmation Bias: A Ubiquitous Phenomenon in Many Guises." *Review of General Psychology* 2, no. 2 (1998).

O'Brien, Kevin J. "Nokia's Success Bred Its Weakness; Stifling Bureaucracy Led to Lack of Action on Early Smartphone Innovation." *International Herald Tribune*, September 27, 2010.

Olson, Matthew S., Derek van Bever, and Seth Verry. "When Growth Stalls." *Harvard Business Review*, March 2008.

Porter, Michael E. "What Is Strategy?" *Harvard Business Review*, November–December 1996.

Sandström, Christian. "When Digital Imaging Displaced Kodak Film." Gothenburg, Sweden: Chalmers University of Technology, July 16, 2009.

Spear, Steven, and H. Kent Bowen. "Decoding the DNA of the Toyota Production System." *Harvard Business Review,* September–October 1999.

Stewart, Thomas A., and Julia Kirby. "The Institutional Yes—An Interview with Jeff Bezos." *Harvard Business Review*, October 2007.

Stroup, Jim. "Fatal and Futile Fads." *Managing Leadership*, November 18, 2008.

Taylor, Andy. "Driving Smoothly." *BusinessWeek*, January 23, 2008.

Teo, Anna. "SIA's Success Secret Is a Tough Balancing Act." *Business Times*, July 29, 2010.

Thompson, Fred. "Business Strategy and the Boyd Cycle." *Journal of Contingencies and Crisis Management,* June 1995.

Wats, Robert. "The Good Brick Who Rebuilt LEGO." *Telegraph*, December 17, 2006.

Webteam Wal-Mart Watch. "The End of the Sam Walton Era." *Wal-Mart Watch*, January 15, 2008.

Whitehall, Bruce. "Julian Metcalfe, Passionate Perfectionist." *Food Service Europe*, February 14, 2007.

Index

Acknowledgments

We wish first to thank the executives who opened the doors of their companies and cleared their calendars to share with us their companies' stories and their own insights. These people are among the busiest people in the world, standing at the forefront of industry in a time of great turbulence. Their generosity in helping with this book was enormous, and their voices echo from every page. We give special thanks to Sunny Verghese, CEO of Olam, who has helped us now for nearly a decade, in each book and each stage of our research. Olam's growth path epitomizes The Great Repeatable Model.

Enormous thanks are also due to the partners of Bain & Company for more than ten years of support for our work on the topic of how companies find their next wave of profitable growth. For *Repeatability*, well over two hundred partners contributed case examples, read and commented on the draft, or assisted us in building our master company database. It is a tribute to their generosity and to the team values at the center of the Bain culture. We especially thank Steve Schaubert, whose ideas run like a golden thread through all of our books, and who remains a mentor to us both. Steve has helped us achieve greater understanding of what really works in business.

Phebo Wibbens is the brilliant and creative consultant who guided the key analysis, reacted to each word of every manuscript draft, and served as the daily sparring partner for Chris in Amsterdam on every new thought and piece of data that we developed. Thank you, Phebo. We would also like to thank Anouk Piening for her brilliant analytic support and Jennifer Kim and her strategy practice team for providing amazing behind-the-scenes expertise.

Paul Judge, Wendy Miller, and their superb team in Bain marketing played myriad roles at every stage of the process, from title selection to fast-turnaround reactions on drafts to organizing the digital media platform. We would especially like to thank Maggie Locher, who organized the fact checking and read manuscript after manuscript in the thankless job of nailing down the details. Thank you!

David Champion is the senior editor at Harvard Business Review Press who worked with us on the structure of the book and then on each draft. David was an intellectual locomotive pulling us along with force and brilliance. We also thank Melinda Adams Merino and her Boston-based Harvard team for superbly choreographing the complex process from concept to cover design to final layout, as they have on all of our books.

Our assistants Brenda Davis, Stefanie van Heteren, and Jane King deserve special thanks for keeping us organized and focused, and for all of their work on the logistics of this book.

Finally, we would like to thank our wives, Donna Robinson and Kathy Allen, for an infinite wellspring of advice, psychology, understanding, motivation, humor, and sometimes forgiveness, as we sequestered ourselves in the supremely self-absorbed task of writing a book. We cannot thank you often or emphatically enough.

About the Authors

CHRIS ZOOK is a partner at Bain & Company and cohead of Bain's Strategy practice. Since joining Bain in 1994, Zook has served in a variety of leadership roles, including membership on Bain's management committee and investment committee.

His client work has focused on helping companies find their next wave of profitable growth, and he has worked in a range of industries, including information, healthcare, computers, and venture capital. He is a frequent speaker at global forums, such as the World Economic Forum at Davos, and was named by *The Times* of London as one of the world's fifty most influential business thinkers.

Zook is the author of the bestselling books *Profit from the Core*, *Beyond the Core*, and *Unstoppable*, published by Harvard Business Review Press. He has also written extensively for business publications ranging from academic journals to columns in the *Wall Street Journal* and the *Washington Post*. He has been a guest on TV and radio, including NPR, CNBC, and Bloomberg TV. He is a frequent speaker at a wide range of business forums, including the Forbes Global CEO Conference, the BusinessWeek CEO Summit, the Economist Summit, the Harvard Burning Questions Conference, and the Harvard Distinguished Speaker Series.

A graduate of Williams College, with advanced degrees in economics from Exeter College, Oxford University, and Harvard University, Zook has a wife and family and divides his time between homes in Amsterdam and Boston.

JAMES ALLEN is a partner in Bain & Company's London office and cohead of Bain's Strategy practice. He joined Bain in 1989, was director of Bain's Moscow office from 1991–95, and has served on Bain's management committee and operating committee.

With more than twenty years of consulting experience, Allen has worked extensively for global companies in consumer products, oil and gas, technology and telecommunications, healthcare, and other industries. He has advised clients on the development of global growth strategies, emerging market entry strategies, and turnaround strategies. As director of Bain Moscow, Allen advised Russian and Eastern European governments, the World Bank, and other agencies on privatization and helped to guide the leadership teams of oil and gas companies on corporate strategy and restructuring issues.

Coauthor of the bestselling book *Profit from the Core*, Allen has written numerous articles on the topics of growth strategy, customer strategy, and the consumer of 2020. He is a frequent speaker at the World Economic Forum and other conferences.

A graduate of Harvard Business School, Allen lives in London with his wife and their children.